BASICS

FASHION DESIGN

09

DESIG
ACCE   IES

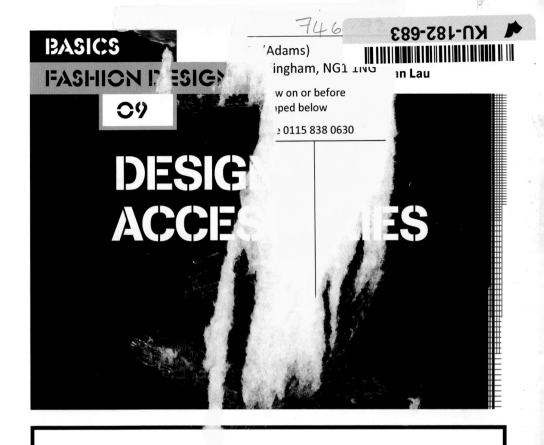

n Lau

Ethical: awareness/ reflection/ ion/ debate

ava
academia

An AVA Book
Published by AVA Publishing SA
Rue des Fontenailles 16
Case Postale
1000 Lausanne 6
Switzerland
Tel: +41 786 005 109
Email: enquiries@avabooks.com

Distributed by Thames & Hudson (ex-North America)
181a High Holborn
London WC1V 7QX
United Kingdom
Tel: +44 20 7845 5000
Fax: +44 20 7845 5055
Email: sales@thameshudson.co.uk
www.thamesandhudson.com

Distributed in the USA & Canada by:
Ingram Publisher Services Inc.
1 Ingram Blvd.
La Vergne TN 37086
USA
Tel: +1 866 400 5351
Fax: +1 800 838 1149
Email: customer.service@ingrampublisherservices.com

English Language Support Office
AVA Publishing (UK) Ltd.
Tel: +44 1903 204 455
Email: enquiries@avabooks.com

© AVA Publishing SA 2012

ISBN 978-2-940411-31-3

Library of Congress Cataloguing-in-Publication Data
Lau, John.
Basics Fashion Design 09: Designing Accessories / John Lau p.cm.
Includes bibliographical references and index.
ISBN: 9782940411313 (pbk. :alk. paper)
eISBN: 9782940439720
1. Dress accessories – Design. 2. Fashion design -- Study and teaching.
GT596 .L38 2012

10 9 8 7 6 5 4 3 2 1

Design by www.studioink.co.uk

Production by AVA Book Production Pte. Ltd., Singapore
Tel: +65 6334 8173
Fax: +65 6259 9830
Email: production@avabooks.com.sg

Jean Paul Gaultier was inspired
by modern Japanese styles for
this handbag (Spring/Summer
2012 haute couture), which
shimmers with layers of large
red sequins, contrasting with
the model's eccentric colours
and style.

Anatomy of accessory

Contents

4 5 6

Accessories are extensions of the body – detachable components that can be used to protect, hide or boast. Accessories are influential symbols that represent the wearer's identity, but when not in use they must stand alone, requiring a powerful presence in order to seduce. *Designing Accessories* explores how designers have evolved from specialist craftspeople to become style leaders in the twenty-first century, who today claim a commanding presence within the fashion industry.

Chapter 1 examines bag, footwear, jewellery and millinery design by exploring the components that make up each piece and providing an overview of how each one connects. We explore each accessory's history, including an object's origins and key developments that have influenced it.

The complete design process, from generating concepts and ideas into key products, is explained in Chapter 2. This process begins with research, a fundamental skill that the designer needs to explore in order to build their knowledge, and which underpins strong design concepts and creative solutions.

Each of the key accessories discussed necessitates the use of various equipment and in Chapter 3, we look at essential tools of the trade and explore two- and three-dimensional construction techniques.

Chapter 4 looks at natural and synthetic materials, and explores which of these delivers the best creative solutions to technical challenges you may be faced with. Once equipped with this knowledge, a designer will have endless resources with which to create excellent products.

Chapter 5 explores traditional and modern, hand- and machine-finishing techniques. The skilful techniques used in accessory design make this discipline distinct from other industries. Traditional hand-finishing techniques give each piece unique characteristics, whilst using machinery can enable a designer to break new boundaries in embellishment techniques.

Eyewear, scarves, belts and gloves are the focus of Chapter 6. These accessories are often viewed as an important complement to a designer's collection. Eyewear is fashionable not only to those who medically require glasses; scarves in a wide range of materials and design are worn throughout the year; belts have an additional function as a design statement; and gloves play both a functional and aesthetic role in the modern wardrobe.

Designing Accessories is also full of interviews with high-profile international designers, who reveal their design processes and the thinking behind them, giving you exclusive insights into the inspirational world of creating accessories. Enjoy the book – and your career in this growing, exciting and influential industry!

This model shows the complete design and construction process that each designer will use to realize their accessories, beginning with research, from concept to consumer.

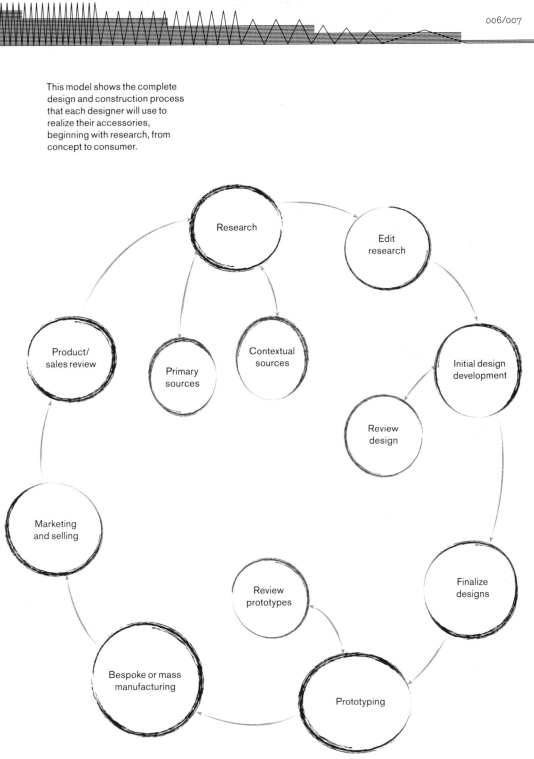

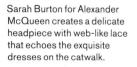

Sarah Burton for Alexander
McQueen creates a delicate
headpiece with web-like lace
that echoes the exquisite
dresses on the catwalk.

An accessory is an object that is worn on the body or carried by a person, yet is completely independent of the user. This powerful extension of the human form comes in thousands of different types of objects; generally speaking, however, the four main forms of accessories are the bag, footwear, jewellery and millinery.

For thousands of years, craftspeople, designers, artisans and makers have honed their knowledge and skills to develop increasingly sophisticated accessories. Accessories were no doubt invented to sustain or facilitate life; the invention of bags enabled food to be carried from place to place, whilst footwear was created to wrap the feet and so enable people to withstand the vagaries of working life. But accessories are also created to show the magnificence of the wearer; richly decorated hats emphasize status, whilst jewellery is often displayed to demonstrate wealth.

Today, the need to sustain life and desire to show magnificence through the use of accessories continues to drive their popularity. Accessories design must therefore balance practical requirements with aesthetic considerations: accessories are increasingly becoming both key fashion items and fashion statements that demand attention as much from those wearing them as from those observing them.

From originally working as craftspeople, accessories designers have developed into today's twenty-first century style leaders. Now working at the forefront of the fashion industry, it is vital that accessories designers have a sound knowledge of the main products from which other styles derive. This chapter looks at the key styles that exist within each category, exploring the details of the core components that make up each type of accessory.

Bags are divided into three categories: the framed bag, inset bag and turned bag. For footwear, the subtle differences between the dress shoe, boot and sport shoe are explained. For jewellery, we will look at the intricate components of the necklace, brooch and ring. Finally the hat and cap, from which all millinery styles are adapted, are explored in this chapter.

This general introduction is designed to provide you with an understanding of the industry and to give you the knowledge that you need to successfully create your own beautiful accessories.

1. The English model and actress Jean Shrimpton in the 1960s, wearing an elaborate tribal-inspired necklace with matching earrings and bracelet made from beads and semi-precious stones.

What is an accessory > The bag

Historically the dominant accessory for men, the bag today has both transcended its modest beginnings and evolved into a must-have, key accessory for women. Bags, especially handbags, have also significantly become a potent symbol of both wealth and power. Most bags basically consist of pieces of leather or fabric that are stitched together with attached hardware or components to make the accessory functional. However, bag design has become increasingly complicated as designers endeavour to differentiate their work from each other in a highly competitive marketplace, and now employs a much wider use of components and logos than ever before.

2. From the Dior Autumn/Winter 2007/8 collection, John Galliano takes inspiration from knotting and applies the bold technique on a solid crocodile leather frame bag.

The historical development of bags

Bags are essentially designed to carry objects. Prior to the twentieth century, bags were used simply to carry essential items or to make a statement of wealth. Women carried needlework in bags when visiting other people in their homes on social occasions, along with other small items such as the calling card and a small bottle of perfume. In addition, small, embroidered bags were carefully made because beautiful handicrafts were an important part of women's domestic lives. However, as needlework fell out of favour over time, other items soon took its place.

The beginning of the twentieth century saw fashions dramatically change. Along with a slimmer silhouette for clothing came the dilemma of how to carry objects that once easily fitted into sleeves and pockets. During the World Wars, the dominance of bags as the main accessory in women's wardrobes occurred as a consequence of them taking up for the first time what were formerly male roles in the workforce – the men having been dispatched to war.

Today, handbags have further increased in size as the modern woman contends with carrying a whole host of portable items together on a daily basis, such as the laptop computer, mobile telephone, cosmetics, diary and other personal effects. This abundance of necessary objects that women need to carry around with them has now spurred a subgenre of bags to hold specific items; or bags may be subdivided for the specific purpose of carrying these items. Due to the decline in the number of men using bags on a daily basis, the style of bags designed for men has seen little progression over the last century; however, the androgynous sports bag, rucksack and messenger bag are now commonplace. This chapter will now turn to focus on three key styles of bags from which most other styles derive: the frame bag, inset bag and turned bag.

Anatomy of an accessory

The frame bag

Some bags are named after specific job roles that they are designed to accompany or assist, such as the doctor's bag, or 'frame bag'. To hold contents securely, a bag can make use of a frame to withstand the carried objects' heavy weight. These bags are usually more complicated in their design, style and shape, as they require the designer to work with the hardware components and confines of the existing structure. The frame bag requires the hardware to be both strong enough to hold its internal contents and have a securely fitting enclosure or fastening. By maintaining its defined shape, this type of bag can ultimately withstand heavy-duty use, but will have less flexibility than other designs due to its somewhat rigid structure.

3. A frame bag designed by Arnoldo][Battois that shows the key components required to complete the accessory.

4. A sleek design by Jil Sander takes inspiration from vintage 1950s styling in this modern variation of a frame bag for Spring/Summer 2012.

3

Handle

Frame closure

Gusset

Side panel

The frame bag deconstructed

Side panel
A large piece of fabric or leather that is usually backed by a stiff canvas or material to hold the shape of the bag together.

Gusset
The side panel that makes a bag larger by discreetly expanding the sides, or smaller by gently folding inwards.

Frame closure
The main solid-frame hardware of the bag, which is made from metal or another rigid material and which can be securely closed with a snap fastening or lock.

Handle
Varying in lengths to enable it to be either worn around the arm or to be held by the hand.

Lining (hidden)
A hard-wearing material that protects the inside of the bag and may also lend it some structure.

Anatomy of an accessory

The inset bag 5

The increasing ease of travel from the 1840s onwards began to radically alter the design of bags. Bags became larger to enable people to carry more and more objects around the world with them, and softer bags allowed the contents within more flexibility of space and were so designed for ease of handling. The inset bag has since become a hugely popular style, being both flexible and expandable, so fitting well into modern women's lifestyles. The inset bag can be shaped by the cut of the panels, gusset and base.

Anatomy of an accessory

5. Gucci uses bright jewel-tone leathers for these 1940s-inspired inset-style handbags.

The inset bag deconstructed

Side panel
A large piece of fabric or leather that can be backed by a stiff canvas to hold the shape of the bag or which may be softly backed for flexible shaping.

Gusset
The side panel that makes a bag larger by expanding the sides, or smaller by gently folding inwards.

Base
The defining piece of this bag is the base panel that provides structure and stability to the accessory.

Handle
A hard-wearing and rigid handle that is carried on the hand or arm.

Enchapes
These are attached to the handle buckles to provide reinforcement and stability.

Pocket (hidden)
These can appear both on the inside and outside of a bag and in a range of sizes, and are generally designed to segregate objects.

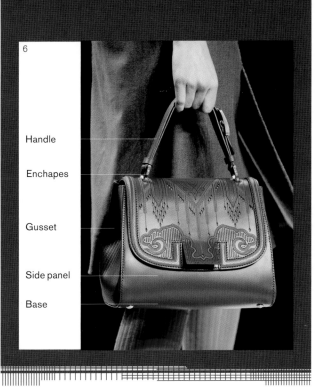

6

Handle

Enchapes

Gusset

Side panel

Base

6. A structured inset-style handbag with intricate tribal-inspired cut-out detailing on the flap by Fendi, which shows the key components required to complete the accessory.

The turned bag

Turned bags can be considered one of the first styles of bags. This basic bag developed from the reticule, a simple bag that served the function of a pocket in the eighteenth and nineteenth centuries. The small pocket, made of silk and often net, beading or brocade, had a cord thread around the neck of the bag that was pulled tight to secure its contents. At their most basic, the side panels are sewn together and the bag is 'turned' right-side out, thereby hiding the seams. Being the most versatile bags, they can be worn with a long or short strap or may be carried with a handle.

7. A leather turned bag from Paul Smith's Spring/Summer 2012 collection that shows the key components required to complete a turned bag.

8. A fur and leather turned bag from Bottega Veneta's Autumn/Winter 2011 collection.

7

Shoulder strap

Ram rings

Front panel

The turned bag deconstructed

Shoulder strap
This long strap can vary in length and enables a bag to be worn either over the shoulder or across the body.

Ram rings
These are circular metal rings used to hold the shoulder strap securely to the bag so providing flexibility of movement.

Front panel
This is folded over the front to protect the interior contents of the bag.

Anatomy of an accessory

In modern times, just as in the past, footwear subtly gives away secrets about the identity of its wearer. But basic footwear has changed relatively little in comparison to other aspects of the fashion industry, from shoes worn day-to-day, to boots that protect the wearer against the elements, to sports shoes made with all the latest technological advances.

Essentially, shoes have three main component parts: the upper, the soles, and the heels. Leather or fabric is layered and stitched to create a moulded shape over a sole and heel to fit the foot.

9. Heavily embellished shoes by Alexander McQueen (Spring/Summer 2008), which cut a dramatic shape with their sculpted platform base.

10. This shoe design by Rodarte is inspired by blue and white Chinese porcelain: its heavy wedge heel is inspired by antique wood carvings.

9

The development of footwear

From their origins as gentle craftspeople, shoemakers have developed to become designers who utilize research into the science, technology and engineering of the design and manufacturing of shoes. Some early guilds of shoemakers, such as the Worshipful Company of Cordwainers in London, UK, still exist today to nurture and promote young talent in the fashion and shoemaking industries.

One of the most important sources of inspiration influencing the history of footwear design has been history itself. The actual shapes used in footwear design have changed relatively little, however, except for when scales of component parts have been exaggerated.

Historically, footwear has been hugely important in separating both classes and cultures. For example, medieval Europe imposed height and decorative restrictions on footwear, and in pre-modern China tiny women's shoes were made to fit women's bound feet. Such limitations had a significant impact on social structures, in a way that is not seen as often – or as dramatically – today. Mobility, for instance, was radically impacted upon, as the higher classes tended to wear shoes that made working, or even walking, difficult.

Although fashion has played an important part in the engineering of footwear design, utility and comfort are also crucial factors. The practicality of the design is a key demand in modern footwear, the vast majority of which is designed to meet a need. However, designers have continually pushed the limits of design by including designer touches and embellishments to make shoes noticeable on the runway or in the street.

10

> '**Shoes make a woman.**'
> Manolo Blahnik

The dress shoe

In this section, we dissect the dress shoe in order to see clearly the components that constitute it, providing a view of how each connects in an easily comprehensible way.

11. A men's leather dress shoe with brogue styling.

11

Counter
This area covers the back of the shoe and is generally stiff to withstand hard wearing.

Quarter
The side panel below the topline under the ankle.

Topline
The edge along the opening of the shoe.

Tongue
This is put in place to provide comfort for the wearer.

Heel
A low heel that can be made out of a variety of strong materials including wood, rubber or plastic.

Shank
A shaped area to provide support underfoot.

Men's dress shoe

Men's dress shoes can be very complicated, with many component parts. These parts are often decorative or embellished with perforated holes, known as 'brogueing', and serrated edges on the leather uppers.
The history of this type of shoe can be traced back to its Scottish and Irish roots.
The perforations, which are now decorative, were once functional to allow for water to escape when the shoe became wet.

There are many different styles of dress shoe, including the wingtip, longwing, semi and quarter, which have in turn inspired women's shoe design. Once considered an outdoor shoe, they have now become commonplace in all social and business occasions.

Shoelaces
These are designed to hold the centre front closed and keep the shoe in place.

Vamp
A panel that covers the side of the shoe.

Toe box
This area is reinforced to protect the toes.

Toe cap
The style of the shoe is determined by the shaping of this area.

Sole
The bottom supporting component of the shoe.

Welt
Where the uppers meet the sole of the shoe.

The bag > **Footwear** > Jewellery

Women's dress shoe

The women's court shoe tends to be less complicated with fewer component parts. One piece of leather can be carefully crafted and moulded into a single shape. The major difference in the design of women's shoes, compared to that of men's, are the variations in heel shape and size that are available to the designer.

The length of the heel can be at any height, as the only limits to the design are the safety and comfort of the wearer. The range of heel shapes – platform, wedge, kitten, cone or puppy heel – in conjunction with the design of the shoe, can produce an almost limitless number of styles.

12

Quarter
The side area below the top line under the ankle.

Breast
The top of the heel meeting the sole of the shoe.

Shank
A shaped area to provide support underfoot.

Heel
A wide range of lengths, shapes and styles made from a variety of materials.

Lift
A guard piece to protect the heel against the ground.

Sole
A solid piece of material along the underside of the shoe.

12. A high-heeled patent leather women's dress shoe.

'I don't know who invented high heels, but all women owe him a lot!'
Marilyn Monroe

Top line
The edge along the opening of the shoe.

Vamp
Side panel of the shoe.

Throat
The front section of the top line opening.

Toe
The area is reinforced to protect the toes.

The bag > **Footwear** > Jewellery

The boot

Boots are designed for warmth and heavy-duty activity. Riding boots have been an important feature in history because of their centuries of continual use for travelling. Special boots were designed for designated jobs, such as metal toecaps for the military and simple, moulded, rubber wellington boots for gardening.

In the nineteenth century, women wore boots in both summer and winter. The boots were generally made of fine materials in lace or calf leather. They were eventually reserved almost exclusively for wearing during cold weather.

Boots only became fashionable slowly over the twentieth century. The largest growth in popularity came with the rise of hemlines in the 1960s, with examples extending to the thigh. During this time, experimentation with materials was driven by the use of innovations that supplemented the mainstay, leather. Rubber, plastic and other synthetics also became increasingly popular.

13. Laced boots by Sarah Burton for Alexander McQueen, from the Autumn/Winter 2011 collection.

Different types of boots

Cavalry jackboots, Chelsea, combat, Courrèges, Cowboy, desert, go-go, granny, hiking, mukluk, pixie, riding, ski, snow, walking, wellington and workmen's.

14. High-heeled leather boot
by Lara Bohinc.

14

Top line
The edge of the
boot opening.

Vamp
A panel that
covers the side
of the boot.

Counter
This hard-wearing
area covers the
back of the boot.

Quarter
The side panel
below the ankle.

Heel
A heel is made
from a variety of
strong materials
including wood,
plastic and metal.

Shank
A shaped area to
provide support
underfoot.

The bag > **Footwear** > Jewellery

The sports shoe

A shoe with a rubber sole was said to have been developed in the nineteenth century in the United Kingdom as a means for the police to sneak up on thieves without being heard – a somewhat humble start to the worldwide phenomenon of the sports shoe! Early sports shoes were made from excess rubber that was left over from manufacturing other products. Today, the sports shoe is a globally recognizable accessory that transcends cultures, ages, genders and personalities. Athletes were the first to notice the benefits of using sports shoes to run faster or jump higher, but what this accessory means to modern culture is far more influential.

From international sportswear brands to fashion designers on the runway, the industry's use of rubber, plastics and synthetic fibres has now been fully incorporated into the mainstream.

15. A typical sports shoe showing its complex design and technologically advanced components.

15

Tongue
Provides support for the wearer and is an area on which companies typically concentrate their branding.

Ankle collar
A section that is reinforced to support the ankle.

Side panel
This is often another area of the sports shoe where companies concentrate their branding.

Heel
The most cushioned part of the sports shoe is highly developed for the wearer's comfort.

Midsole
Between the upper and outsole, this has been an important section where technological advances have been focused.

Anatomy of an accessory

Sports shoe development

The combination of design and colour can bring together a huge number of possibilities for a designer, and the design of the sports shoe has developed immensely over the past century. There has been a huge leap forward from the simple canvas and rubber-sole sports shoes that athletes used to rely on. The classic sports shoe took visual clues from existing footwear, with plain lines of design and construction. Modern sports shoes take their inspiration from many cues, such as colour, style line, materials, or even a sports personality. Today, companies continually release more than one model in a range of colourways.

Usually being subject to high wear and tear in professional sports, the design process also takes into consideration the end user's requirements. Technology has advanced sports shoe design with better synthetics being continually developed. The methods of production have progressed too, harnessing the potential of machinery, such as injection moulding. There are four main types of sports shoes, including: low-tops, which do not cover the ankle; high-tops, which cover the ankle; mid-cuts are in between the low-tops and high-tops; and sneaker boots, which generally extend to the calf. As sports shoes have today become a fashion item, the design elements of the shoe can be balanced in favour of the practical.

Toe box
This area is well-ventilated to prevent the build-up of heat, keeping the wearer cool during intensive use.

Outsole
This is a piece of rubber that must be hard wearing and adapted to the specific sport/activity.

Forefoot
The special grooves underneath the sports shoe are designed to grip to a range of surfaces.

Useful terms

The sports shoe is a recognizable, dominant accessory across the globe and every culture has developed their own unique names to refer to it. Other terms in popular use today are: athletic shoe, baskets, gym boots, joggers, runners, running shoes, sneakers, tackies, trainers and turnschuhe.

The bag > **Footwear** > Jewellery

Jewellery

Jewellery consists of many decorative and functional components varying widely in size and functional capabilities. The flexibility of component parts makes this type of accessory dynamic, as many can be interchangeable, although some are exclusive to a particular type. The landscape of jewellery design has changed with commercial demands, but the basics of manufacturing, building layers, and linking chains and attaching pieces remains the same. Even with automated manufacturing, constructing jewellery continues to be a lengthy, hands-on process.

The development of jewellery

The earliest jewellery to have been discovered to date heralds from around 20,000 BC and was unearthed in an area that now forms the border regions of modern-day Iran, Iraq, Syria and Turkey. The materials used in early jewellery were shell, bone, ivory and wood, that may have been found or left over from other more valuable products.

The most significant evolution in jewellery design occurred around the fifth century. The Greeks expanded the use of materials used to include precious metals and stones. Different types of jewellery then began to emerge, including pendants, bracelets, rings and brooches. At the same time, the Far East – especially China – was developing its use of jade in jewellery design, along with its own inimitable style.

The rise in popularity of using gold, silver and precious stones has led to them becoming the mainstay of jewellery design ever since. Intricate designs in early jewellery, such as engraving and cutwork, eventually gave way to increasingly larger precious stones. Excavating these precious stones became easier as the technology for extracting them advanced.

There are many famous stones, including the Hope Diamond, also known as 'Le bleu de France' or 'Le Bijou du Roi'. The Cullinan diamond was the largest rough gem-quality diamond ever found, from which the largest polished gem from the stone is Cullinan 1 or the Great Star of Africa. This was superseded in size in 1985 by the discovery of the Golden Jubilee diamond, which was found in the same mine. The Great Star of Africa and the Golden Jubilee form part of the collection of the crown jewels of the United Kingdom and Royal Thai Palace respectively.

Affordable jewellery using precious metals later became available for the masses with the discovery of electroplating base metals with thin layers of gold and silver. Many types of materials are now used in fashion jewellery. Chanel routinely used semi-precious stones in her jewellery designs and Paco Rabanne paved the way in making the use of plastic acceptable. Cheaper materials create larger costume jewellery that can make a more dramatic statement.

We will now explore the three key items of jewellery design – the necklace, ring and brooch – and the main components that make up these intricate accessories.

16

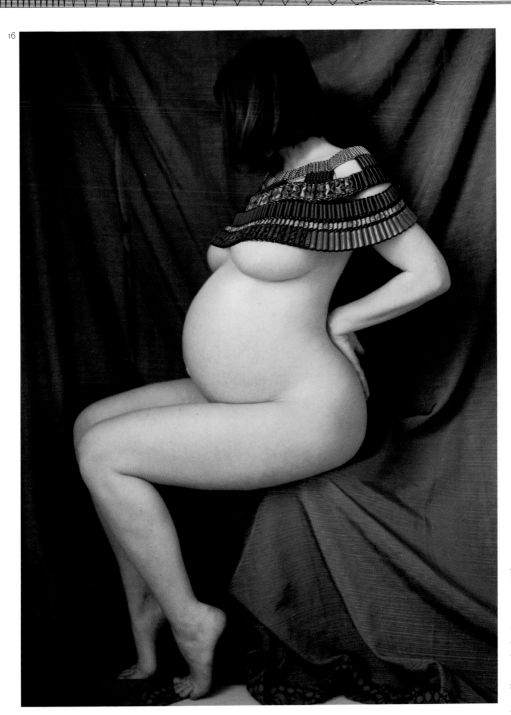

16. Michelle Lowe-Holder uses intense primary colours for this oversized Egyptian-style necklace, which echoes the magnificence of the jewellery worn by the Pharaohs.

The necklace

The earliest humans quickly became adept at stringing together basic materials. The Egyptians, taking advantage of the abundance of materials available in their gold and stone mines, soon began setting stones and linking chains. Craftspeople, inspired by religious symbols and meanings, created intricate designs with engravings into metal.

Today, necklaces can be classed by their design. A chain with a drop will have a pendant or locket attached and one with details that are integrated within the chain will have chain links. Necklaces also vary in lengths – the choker, for instance, is worn tightly fitted around the neck; ropes, on the other hand, are very long and can be wrapped around the wearer's neck several times in order to create the illusion of several necklaces being worn at once.

17. A heavy necklace with a large drop made with several rings by contemporary jewellery designer Scott Wilson.

18. A multi-coloured stone necklace by Balenciaga (Autumn/Winter 2008) that fuses a modern abstract style with natural materials.

17

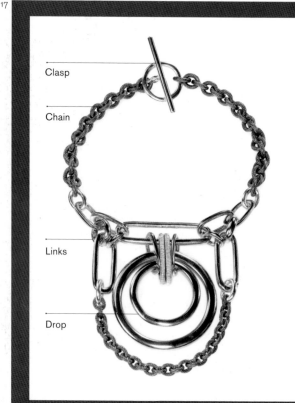

Clasp

Chain

Links

Drop

The necklace deconstructed

Chain
A functional component worn around the neck, which holds other pieces such as a pendant, locket or decorative links.

Clasp
A functional component designed to allow the wearer to open and close the fastening.

Links
These can be used as a decorative component or be purely functional in order to hold together the chain or other pieces within the design, such as a pendant.

Drop
A pendant or locket in varying sizes attached to the main necklace.

The ring

The ring can be considered to be one of the most personal of all accessories. Arguably the most symbolic of all rings is the showcase engagement ring, which has for many generations been a powerful symbol representing a man and a woman's promise to each other to enter into the sacred institution of marriage. The wedding ring is thus another important and significant ring for both women and men. Dress rings, on the other hand, are often large and bulky, and tend to be designed as statement jewellery. Although they are out of fashion today, funeral or memorial rings were once widely distributed to commemorate a death in the latter half of the seventeenth century.

Yet rings can be some of the most complicated pieces of jewellery to make because of the size and intricacy of the design work, especially with regards to the settings for holding stones for instance.

Ring shank

Setting

Anatomy of an accessory

Useful terms

Ring shank
The band, usually in metal, that fits around the finger.

Setting
The component that holds an item, such as a stone, in place.

19. A knuckleduster-style ring from Chanel's Autumn/ Winter 2011 collection.

20. A contemporary diamond ring with a set stone.

The brooch

The first brooch was developed from the ancient fibula, which was a functional accessory that held clothing together and was first seen during the Bronze Age. This was the earliest form of a decorative safety pin, using materials such as metals and stones. As they became less functional, brooches developed to become more decorative pieces and the types of materials used to make them subsequently varied to include ceramic, fabric and plastic. The main components, however, have always remained the same. The generally non-functional body of the brooch is the decorative highlight of the accessory. Brooches that are more complicated in design may employ springs and hinges to help with the functionality of the piece in terms of improving its flexibility.

21. Large stones adorn this oversized brooch that acts as both statement jewellery and a functional piece as seen in Givenchy's Spring/Summer 2009 haute couture collection.

21

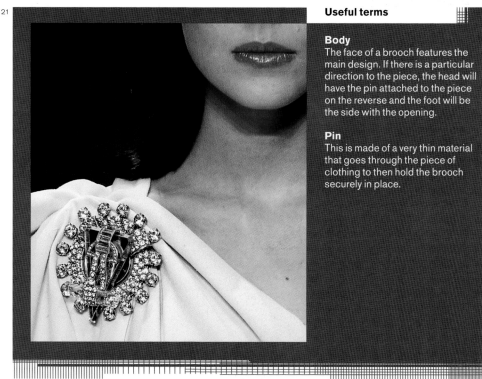

Useful terms

Body
The face of a brooch features the main design. If there is a particular direction to the piece, the head will have the pin attached to the piece on the reverse and the foot will be the side with the opening.

Pin
This is made of a very thin material that goes through the piece of clothing to then hold the brooch securely in place.

22

23

Anatomy of an accessory

Georgina Martin is a jewellery designer who set up her own label in 2006 and focuses on intricate designs. Her designs have been exhibited in galleries and have garnered critical acclaim. All of her designs have stories that are integral to explaining each piece of jewellery; a personalization that connects the wearer with the piece. Georgina's handmade jewellery has been described as totally unique and wonderfully different.

Where do you find inspiration?

My inspiration comes from a wide variety of sources, which can be anything from museums, galleries or stately homes to the world around me. I like my work to tell a story or hold a scene that then becomes encapsulated within the work. From a young age I was taken around stately homes, which I grew to love and appreciate. I would find the stuffed animals set in scenes behind glass repulsive but intriguing, the decadent furniture would be covered in ornate patterns adding to the grandeur of the houses. I also find inspiration in Victorian jewellery that tells romantic messages through stones and lockets that hold the hair of lost ones.

How do you start a new collection?

When I start a new collection, I aim to design a piece that I would wear and that will inspire me to be creative. This might be a ring, necklace or brooch and is not always intended for sale. From this main design, I take elements that can then be translated into a collection; this will usually incorporate a necklace, two sets of earrings and a bracelet. I really love making brooches as these can be larger or more ornate than other elements of a collection, so I try to add these in too.

How do you organize your research?

I have a hectic system of organization, with multiple sketchbooks being used at once and then the finalization of designs done on large sheets of paper. Large sheets allow me to draw variations together and also to scale, so I can assess the best design. I make models and samples during the design process, letting the materials develop the design.

What is your design process?

I sometimes set myself a brief, which could be a word, theme or object. I collect images or objects that I find inspiring based on the brief.

24

25

From these I start to draw elements, focusing on shape, texture, forms or colour. These then lead me through to a possible design. I find it much easier to make models and samples alongside the design stage, using copper or brass, in a few cases silver too.

Once I have finalized the design, I start making the pieces in silver. There will often be changes at this stage too; surface finish and scale are the elements played with most. The completed prototype allows me to work out making time, material costs and changes in the construction process to make the process more cost-effective.

What types of jewellery do you design?

Mainly rings and necklaces, but also earrings and bracelets. Lockets will always be close to what I do because I aim to create a narrative with my jewellery. They have the flexibility to hold so much in such a small area. The romance of lockets will always be there as, although they are seen as historical pieces, they can be very contemporary items.

What types of materials do you use?

Mainly silver because of the flexibility of the metal. It can have a variety of finishes including polished, patina, enamelling, satin and brushed, but I also find the incorporation of non-precious metals inspiring too. Copper has such possibilities for natural surface finishes; using heat and patinas can really bring a piece to life with an injection of colour. By being selective, I ensure that a constant standard is achieved across my collections.

What advice do you have for new designers?

Start with a single range: a concentrated range really reflects you as a designer. Always get feedback from your stockists as this is invaluable in creating future ranges. Finally, knowing who you are designing for is key to the success of any designer.

22–25. The wearer needs to look closely at Georgina Martin's intricate pieces to fully appreciate the magical tiny cut-outs in silver encased in lockets and in rings.

Jewellery > Industry perspective> Millinery

All hats are derived from two basic styles, the hat and cap, brimmed and brimless. Both types are resourceful in their practical function of protecting the head, as even elaborate headwear must be shaped to fit well. In modern times, hats have become much less commonplace and are generally reserved for special occasions. Men were originally the main wearers of millinery, but as with most accessories, hats too have since become dominated by women's styles.

Sports headwear is also an important part of the industry today, whether required by sportsmen and women or as a fashion product. Another area that cannot be overlooked is protective headwear, which is an essential part of the uniform for the police, soldiers and chefs, as well as for other specific job roles.

The development of millinery

In Milan, during the mid-sixteenth century, importers of haberdashery and the highly sought-after straw hat were known as 'millaners', which eventually evolved into the modern word 'milliner' that we use today. However, the idea of headwear goes far back into history, with the creation of basic hats fashioned from the simplest of materials to grand styles displaying the power and wealth of the wearer. In England during the early to mid-twentieth century, for instance, an upper-class man would have worn a top hat, whilst a man from the working classes would have worn a bowler hat or flat cap.

Historically, there were clear rules to wearing hats. It was common for women to wear them indoors, although hats were usually worn by men and many styles today have drawn inspiration from men's styles. The beginning of the twentieth century saw the rise in dominance of Paris and haute couture in millinery. Couturiers dismantled barriers by creating fashionable millinery from styles that were previously associated with the working classes; the prime example of this being Christian Dior, who created a conical straw hat, also known as a 'coolie' hat for his collection in 1947.

The emergence of new types of materials and techniques has made it possible to create complex hats and caps, although the traditional components remain relatively unchanged.

Anatomy of accessory

Many key styles are repeated today, but with increasingly elaborate embellishments. The range of modern materials now available for use in millinery has enabled designers to create more architectural pieces, limited only by their imaginations and by how much the head can hold. The structure of the accessory can be moulded using the traditional hat block or created by building a scaffold without the support of the block. Milliners work closely with designers, usually collaborating on their collections to complement each other's work. As hats are very noticeable on the catwalk, the pieces tend not just to be confined to enhancing an outfit, but often work as standalone pieces.

26. The singer, actress and mistress Lady de Bathe here showcases Edwardian formal dress with an outlandish hat trimmed with fine feathers along the upturned brim.

27. John Galliano for Dior's Spring/ Summer haute couture 2010 collection, which takes inspiration from classical millinery design and crafts a hat with a dramatic swirl of feathers for the brim on a small crown.

The hat

Scales and shapes of hats vary widely and according to fashion, trends and tastes. For example, in medieval times, elaborate hats gave way to functionality, as they became flattened on the sides to accommodate the drawing of the sword. As with most accessories, men's hats led the way in design. This male-dominated area eventually inspired women's hats which, over time, have become the crowning glory of millinery.

The main styles of hats have changed relatively little since their initial designs. However, modern hats do not necessarily require a crown or- brim. The materials used in hat construction have expanded greatly from the basic straw and felt traditionally employed. Today, the number of milliners has fallen dramatically, however, with few outlets creating for the ready-to-wear market, while only a small number design and manufacture exclusively for the haute couture houses in Paris. Some designers have collaborated successfully with clothing designers, although most have their own ranges. Creative milliners make up a small, but highly visible, part of the industry.

28

29

28. Stephen Jones's contemporary take on the perfectly-proportioned beret featuring small details on the crown.

29. The bright magenta highlights the delicate fringe and lace detailing on this variation of a boater, designed by Chanel.

30. A classic piece designed by Stephen Jones, which is adorned with a dramatic flourish of colour.

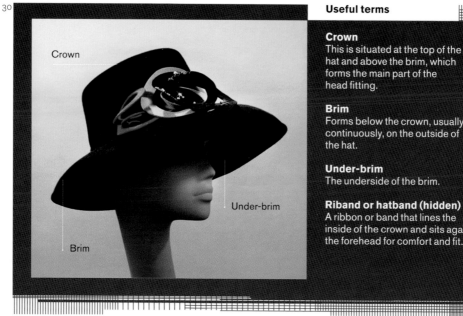

30

Crown

Under-brim

Brim

Useful terms

Crown
This is situated at the top of the hat and above the brim, which forms the main part of the head fitting.

Brim
Forms below the crown, usually continuously, on the outside of the hat.

Under-brim
The underside of the brim.

Riband or hatband (hidden)
A ribbon or band that lines the inside of the crown and sits against the forehead for comfort and fit.

The cap

The cap was originally worn by workmen and was a staple in working-class fashion due to its severe practicality. Today, there are many types of caps, including brimless or brimless with a peak worn over the eyes. The most identifiable style is the baseball cap, which surged in popularity during the 1980s as a key youth accessory and featured distinctive logos, colours and designs. This tightly fitting headwear remains a dominant feature in sportswear and has on occasion become a highly sought-after fashion product. Recently, milliners and couturiers have designed caps made from exquisite fabrics embellished with expensive components, creating headwear that easily competes with the most elaborate accessory.

Types of hats

Boater, bonnet, bowler, cloche, coolie, cowboy, fedora, panama, picture, top hat and trilby.

Types of caps

Baseball, beanie, beret, butcher's boy, fez, field, flat, newsboy, peaked, sailor and skull.

31

31. An oversized silk cap with leopard print by Riccardo Tisci for Givenchy Haute Couture (Autumn/ Winter 2007).

32. A sectional cap designed by Stephen Jones shows a contemporary take on a simple style.

33. An oversized pageboy cap circa 1960s mixes informal and formal styles.

32

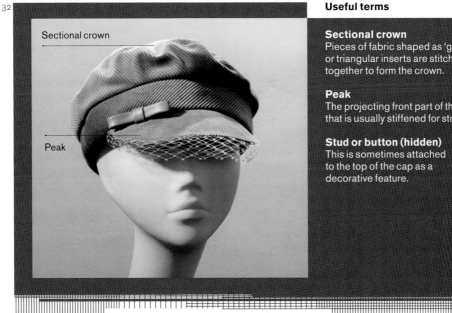

Sectional crown

Peak

Useful terms

Sectional crown
Pieces of fabric shaped as 'gores' or triangular inserts are stitched together to form the crown.

Peak
The projecting front part of the brim that is usually stiffened for strength.

Stud or button (hidden)
This is sometimes attached to the top of the cap as a decorative feature.

33

Philip Treacy

34

35

36

A multi-award-winning milliner who is recognized internationally for his creative designs, Philip Treacy has collaborated with many influential fashion designers, including Karl Lagerfeld and Alexander McQueen. He is known for his sculptural hats, which have adorned the heads of both royalty and the most prominent supermodels. Philip continues to inspire designers within the industry, as well as his celebrity fans, which include Lady Gaga.

What inspires you most in millinery?

I take my inspiration from natural forms and the beautiful lines in nature. I use contemporary influences, be it sculpture or art or whatever is going on in the world today. I always try and do something new and fresh; there is always something new inspiring me. In terms of people, my biggest inspirations are of course my clients.

34–38. A range of Philip Treacy's hats, which show a masterful skill in proportion and use of materials in his contemporary collections – in which feathers, plastic, felt and lace combine to conjure fantasy pieces into reality.

Where does your inspiration originate?

My Irish heritage has had a huge influence on the way I design. My Irishness is part of my being really. What I do is Irish design. It doesn't have any shamrocks on it though! It's twenty-first century Irish fashion. I was always influenced by beauty. At home in Ireland, we were taught about the beauty of nature. I find the natural lines in my work in the contours of the landscape where I grew up. We had lots of chickens, pheasants and geese so the prime ingredient of the hats I make are feathers because I know them very well. Also, my sister Marion was the most glamorous girl in the world. She was a huge inspiration to me. She was my introduction to fashion and magazines. She worked as a nurse in London and used to come home on holidays with all these great magazines like *Harpers* and *Vogue*, which I'd never seen.

What is your design process?

The hats usually start off as drawings. I've been working with a Paris-based block shaper, Renzo Re (La Forme), who transforms three-dimensional shapes, which I then personally create using a material of woven wood and cotton called 'sparterie', into wooden forms. Every hat we make undergoes this process.

Anatomy of an accessory

37

38

How do you develop your shapes?

I use the model as a map, or a key, to carve the actual shape in sparterie; I'm using some measurements, but mostly my eye. In hat making, let me tell you, even a fraction of an inch is crucial. It's all very precise.

How is your colour palette compiled each season?

Every season is different from the past one; we always need something new and different. For this reason, I have straw and felt dyed in the colours I personally find. The colour could come from a real flower, fruit or from a candy shop. It can be anything!

What inspires you most when working on collaborative projects?

It's exciting to work with strong designers because they let you interpret their style. Some designers are specific, but many designers that I have worked with for a long time give me free rein to design with their collections in mind. I have collaborated with Ralph Lauren, Karl Lagerfeld for Chanel, Valentino, Giorgio Armani, and Riccardo Tisci for Givenchy, all of whom have a huge amount of talent.

How do you present your collection?

Twice a year we present the new collection at Premiere Classe in Paris, even if we still have our showroom in London.

Why is millinery an important feature in a fashion collection?

A hat can completely change the personality of the wearer, make them stand differently and walk differently. A hat can make that person feel interesting. A good hat is the ultimate glamour accessory. It thrills observers and makes the wearer feel a million dollars. This creates a high status of desirability and although the images received can seem out of this world, the conspicuous consumer relates strongly to them.

What are the best design techniques a new designer should learn?

There are only ever guidelines to follow, but never rules... you will know through your own judgement when a hat is right... but the most important thing is that the wearer feels happy and confident. Do they smile when they see themselves in the mirror? Do you see a sparkle in their eye? That's when you know you've done it right.

Philip Treacy

39

40

41

42

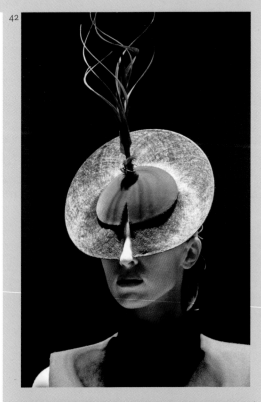

43

39–44. The energy of Philip Treacy's sketches is translated into reality for his catwalk collections. Inspiration – taken from nature and beyond – is used to extraordinary effect for both wearer and viewer.

Anatomy of an accessory

44

Philip Treacy

45

46

45–47. For his collections, Philip Treacy creates drama with the simplest of materials, such as a spectacular sweep of feathers that lightly covers the models' faces. His gently amusing hat designs need no further explanation.

47

Developing an accessories library

All designers must possess an excellent knowledge of many different styles of bags, footwear, jewellery and millinery. This will involve research into what the industry currently offers, together with historical references. This activity should be an ongoing exercise, which will enable you to create a library of information that will fully inform you of the possibilities that exist in accessories design and manufacture. This indispensable guide will then help you to develop confidence in both developing and managing this information into the creation of tangible products.

Objective and learning outcome

The purpose of this activity is to build a foundation of knowledge of the many different types of accessories that exist within the main four categories of accessory design, which can then be used in the design process.

Design task

Start with primary research to develop your knowledge of the current market. This will inform you of the main developments in accessories in the key market areas as these continue to grow according to changing tastes, design and production techniques.

Note down the key style features from the four main categories using this chapter to help name the components. It is important at this stage to differentiate components from embellishments, as the former play an integral part in the workings of the accessory, whilst the latter are purely aesthetic.

Your primary research should then be supplemented with secondary research conducted by reading texts or looking for images in a wide range of media, such as books and websites. This method of research can be very useful in making you aware of distinctive elements that may have fallen out of use in accessory design but which might be successfully revitalized with a revolutionary modern look.

Remember: as you develop your accessories library, you need to create a clear system of filing the information that you have gathered. Make sure that you file your research into subject categories to ensure easy future reference.

48. A complete look with intricate embellishments on the shoes and silk cloche, featured in Chanel's haute couture Autumn/Winter 2009 collection.

48

2

A collection of shoes with a shot
of fluorescent colour, which
highlights the subtle detailing of
the notch cut-out of the high
heels by Costume National
(Spring/Summer 2012).

Before you can begin thinking about researching your initial ideas in preparation for designing your own range of accessories, you first need to develop a good understanding of the design process, which we shall begin exploring in the sections that follow.

What is the design process? Successful design requires a cycle of start and finish points. With each piece of accessory, the designer will need to manage the design for many different products at once in order to produce a coherent range. Throughout the design process, working in a wide range of areas may include working across different styles and market ranges, or perhaps working in collaboration with other designers.

The design process begins by defining the problem and setting a brief. Either the company or designer will set these parameters to ensure that the accessory meets expectations. The brief may depend on the client's needs, such as meeting a customer requirement; or rest on a designer's point of view; or be dependent on constraints set by a company. Each of these situations requires the designer to respond differently to a specific demand.

1. A line sheet shows a mix of sketches and specifications by Jody Parchment.

2. Shoes with a lace-like laser-cut detail by contemporary shoe designer Jody Parchment, inspired by historical research.

1

2

Researching ideas

Researching an idea might have many different sources: ideas can spring from a designer's surroundings; from what is natural or artificial; or from what has come before or an event in the future. Rarely is an idea completely new; most are inspired by something historical or something that has been expressed before. But with each new interpretation of an idea, boundaries become blurred, cross-cultural references are integrated, unknown cultures are discovered, and crucially, social and artistic progression is made.

Now, your amassed research should be critically examined so that you can select the strongest themes from within it. Design ideas should then be developed with quick sketches by the designer or in a team, by fully expanding the research themes into possible accessories designs. During this process, materials should be selected because designs can be limited by what is available, which may also create the need for new developments to suit the accessory being designed.

Finally, the designs will be brought together and every accessory will come together to form a collection. With careful editing, the key pieces will create a successful range that can be made into prototypes and then be taken into production. This chapter introduces the key concepts of the design process and presentation for the accessory designer.

The design process > Doing research

Research is a continual process that can inspire both the immediate project and beyond. Inspiration can be sought and found all around, and is best begun by documenting striking visual imagery – be it fabric swatches and pieces of leather, precious stones or synthetic plastics. Accessories often rely on tiny components to complete a creative outcome. Designers also look to other creative outlets for gathering ideas, for instance literature and art movements, social groups or subcultures. Observing cultural habits and behaviours can also provide inspiration; studying different cultures can broaden your understanding of why and how accessories are worn, in turn inspiring shapes and embellishments.

3. Decorative ironworks adorning windows and the base of a street light in Prague serve as inspiration for Georgina Martin's jewellery designs (see pages 36–7).

3

Developing research themes

Compiling research takes time to fully develop into tangible pieces. Independent ideas that do not immediately match or make sense may take time to nurture. Experimenting alongside thorough investigation can yield new ideas or strengthen existing ones. Research can form in two ways: either creatively with a freestyle compilation of imagery, writings and sampling; or technically, through rigorous documentation of testing and results. Recurring themes will develop as your key research addresses the needs of a particular moment, season and functional requirement. Such themes can be incorporated with a designer's signature style, which users can identify with. The fundamental areas to focus on each time that research is compiled include colour, shape and texture.

Compiling research

Gathering research can define the purpose of a new collection of accessories. A sketchbook is easy to keep and carry, and is useful as a means to keep an ongoing record of both the visuals and notes that you have been pulling together.

Completing research in this format should be built in layers. A strong image may take prominence on a single page, but an intuitive designer will treat it instead as a base to reflect upon whether to build up the theme or whether to deconstruct it for a closer examination of the basic elements. Research into a new collection is highly personal. It is necessary to clarify a vision, refine an idea and to simplify a working concept.

Moodboards

Moodboards tell an overall story by showing a strong theme that presents a coherent concept. They enable a gathering together of the main imagery collected, along with colours, patterns and textures that can then be clearly edited to convey a sense of the collection simply and succinctly. It is important that the format chosen for the moodboard is either large or presented in a way that is easily readable. With computer technology, e-moodboards are easily created and shared. This method of presentation is useful for disseminating ideas to large teams when working on collaborative projects and as a means to encourage others to collate and share information in a working document.

Compiling a research sketchbook

Sketching primary and secondary sources – drawing from memory and on location by sketching surroundings.

Collecting colours, textures and patterns – from many forms that can be from sources of enquiry other than accessories themselves.

Three-dimensional examination – using sketching or photography to visually document natural and man-made shapes.

The design process > Doing research > Types of research

For centuries, designers have benefited from inspiration from other cultures, with royalty in Europe setting trends for accessories seen around the continent. Accessories designers today continue to plunder archives for inspiration. Starting from an historical perspective can inform a new designer of the things that have come before and highlight the accessories that were most popular, as well as suggesting new possibilities that might arise from their rediscovery.

History informs the designer of the main styles that have previously existed and many have used historical influences to create accessories that are both extravagant and modern. Contemporary accessory design that draws on historical inspiration needs to be considered carefully in order to make a piece wearable. Historical features might be explored using modern materials to instead offer a modern interpretation of an older piece, for instance.

4

5

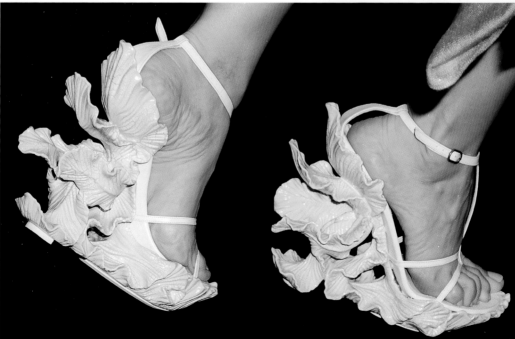

Primary and secondary research will help to develop ideas that can later germinate into common themes and so a proactive designer uses the many resources available to them to conduct effective and relevant research.

Primary research

Primary research requires the designer to go to locations that may yield inspiring information. Visiting museums and art galleries can be extremely valuable for the new designer because such places contain archival evidence of past work. Inspiration should not be limited to accessories, but should also be sought from cultural and artistic movements such as surrealism, for instance, which began in the early 1920s and inspired Elsa Schiaparelli and many other designers of the time.

Primary sources will come from your immediate surroundings and the elements within them, from natural textures to architectural forms. Photography, sketching and collecting visual documentation is crucial in primary research. Although the collected pieces may not immediately suggest a use to you, they may provide a crucial link later with other research elements, so it is worth considering everything carefully. You will need to tread a line between searching for specific information, whilst at the same time remaining open to absorbing your surroundings in order to allow the unexpected to occur or present itself to you.

4. Porcelain of *The Three Graces distressing Cupid*, from the late-eighteenth century.

5. Shoes inspired by white porcelain by Alexander McQueen 2011.

Secondary sources

Secondary research can take on many forms. The Internet has become an excellent tool for archiving work and continues to be supported by published books, magazines, newspapers and an ever-increasing variety of sources. Searching for sources can be easily targeted with the use of key words. However, parameters should be set for a search in order for it to be fruitful as, without it, a designer can gather too much information. Research can start with tear sheets and photocopying, and can move on to digital image manipulation to create specific effects. With careful labelling, an electronic archive is an effective method of keeping stored material for later use.

Research methods

Primary research
Museums, art galleries, towns and cities (for architecture), public events, heritage sites, historical homes, botanical gardens and foreign travel.

Secondary sources for research
Fashion and historical accessories books and archives, artist monographs, fashion and lifestyle magazines, newspapers, industry journals, fashion websites and style blogs.

Doing research > Types of research > Trend forecasting

Contemporary inspirations require the designer to be responsive to trends and to have a keen ability to forecast opportunities from a wide range of sources. Inspiration does not necessarily have to originate from previously produced accessories. Technology has played a key part as a source of contemporary inspiration, especially with the progression of man-made structures, synthetic materials and construction techniques. Computer software can easily create three-dimensional renderings of accessories before they are made. This increased speed and efficiency of product development has had a significant impact on much accessory design, especially in the technological precision of sports footwear. The constant development and refinement of materials has pushed the accessories industry into creating new improvements designed to improve comfort for the wearer.

6. A moodboard by Elin Melin shows inspiration gained from outdoor living. Natural landscapes and vintage tents inspired the design of a leather working bag with functional pockets.

Trends

Trends rely on historical information to inform designers of recurring themes accepted by the general public. The information is collected and analysed to forecast possible upcoming trends that are in the process of developing. The main trends to forecast are colour and style.

Colour

Trend forecasting gives the designer early guidance on changing tastes and styles with the benefit of long-term analysis. The public's taste and willingness to innovate with accessories evolves slowly over a long period of time and it is only on very rare occasions that a new style suddenly emerges. Colour prediction usually takes two years to form because fibres, fabrics and leather are dyed before production. Each country will have representatives meeting to discuss changes in colour before a delegate from each meets with global colleagues to decide on the trends to forecast.

Style

In the fashion industry, there has been a growth in the use of trend researchers called 'cool hunters'. Their task is to seek out new styles from a wide range of sources. The traditional approach to adopting trends has been to observe a trickle-down effect: top designers create innovative accessories, which over time inspires the mass market.

The opposite process of trend adoption is possible too, with influence moving in the opposite direction – what we might call the 'trickle-up' effect. Subcultural trends that originated within distinct social or cultural groups, for instance, can start to inspire the mass market and then be adopted further into the high-end designer market.

Forecasting agencies work to disseminate key themes for the upcoming seasons, although many trends are repeated after a few years in dormancy. Fads surge onto the market buoyed upon a huge rise of popularity, only to disappear as quickly as they appeared. Classic items, however, are fashionable most of the time. For example, the classic Chanel handbag, originally created in the 1920s, remains popular today and continues to inspire a number of contemporary ranges, both within the fashion house from which it originated and by others.

Brainstorming

One effective method of developing ideas is to use brainstorming to expand fully on significant themes. Begin by selecting a key word and finding the primary, secondary and tertiary links to it. Primary links will show direct links; secondary links are indirect; and tertiary links should refer to inspiration that is related to the main theme by loose association.

Using an image instead of a key word can work well when there are many visuals available – a method that is particularly helpful for visual designers. A combination approach might involve the use of text, images, materials, textures and patterns to create a more tactile brainstorm.

Accessories, being usually worn with clothing, play a special role in collaborative partnerships. Accessory and clothing designers, each with their own specialism, will sometimes work in conjunction to create a coherent collection. On the haute couture catwalk, for instance, designers have frequently worked together to complement each other's collections.

Previously, accessories occupied a subordinate role to clothing design, which had the effect of limiting the accessory designer's use of shapes, materials and styles to complement the clothing collection. However, more and more designers have standalone shows where clothing designers are invited to create garments to match the accessories in the collection.

7. This elaborate hat featured in Alexander McQueen's Autumn/Winter 2009–10 collection, created in collaboration with Philip Treacy, which showcases the strength of each designer's work to stunning effect. Philip Treacy's dexterity of the hand turns the hat into a dramatic sculpture of curves and folds, echoing McQueen's oversized ruffled collar on an expertly tailored jacket.

Collaborations enable each designer involved to showcase their designs in an independent but combined effort – such as the brand Alexander McQueen's long-standing relationship with milliner Philip Treacy, for example. Other examples of successful fashion partnerships include Jade Jagger for Garrard; Manolo Blahnik's close work with John Galliano's early Dior haute couture and own-label collections; Karl Lagerfeld's long relationship at Chanel with shoemakers Massaro (which the brand now owns); as well as celebrity partnerships, such as Alexa Chung with Mulberry. Collaborative partnerships can be highly successful in their ability to make an immediate impact, as did the Longchamp Legend bag designed in conjunction with Kate Moss, for example.

Collaborative partnerships can be both intentional and unintentional, as with the Hermès Birkin and Kelly bags – where one was designed in conjunction with the user (actress and singer Jane Birkin) and the other was used often enough for the person to become associated with the accessory (actress Grace Kelly).

Partnerships may also be formed with people who are not part of the fashion industry. There have been many collaborations between fashion and accessory designers with big names from the art world; Stephen Sprouse and Takashi Murakami for Louis Vuitton, Richard Prince for Marc Jacobs and Donna Karan's collection inspired by the Haitian graphic artist Philippe Dodard.

Coordination with clothing

A key factor in accessories design is how well they coordinate with clothing. Each item will be required to play a complementary role, so firstly think about how an accessory will be worn with clothing. Size differences will need to be considered because of issues with fit and the space required to accommodate an accessory. The weight of an accessory must also be taken into account to ensure that its interaction with clothing is not uncomfortable or even dangerous to the wearer.

Creative product development

To generate ideas, select the main reference points from your research and gather the information together into groups, connecting together style, shapes, materials and texture themes. This stage is designed to help you quickly draft out an outline of potential designs by fully utilizing the reference points to examine and extend the details. Sketches will help you to develop stronger themes and, although some limitations may be imposed, generating ideas is the best time to explore the potential of all designs. The commercial market may introduce further limits due to the perceived sales potential of an accessory; bespoke pieces can therefore be limiting because of the customer's specific requirements and ideas. Highlight the key themes and strong ideas that occur in the research that you have collected. Carefully consider merging ideas, such as by updating the design of an historical piece of jewellery to something that is more contemporary, or by redefining the shape of a bag.

Sketching

Confidence in sketching can be achieved by drawing from accessories, which will develop your skills in rendering proportion, shape and perspective: practice makes for continuous improvement. Design ideas are best generated on large sheets of paper that show your development work and the thought processes involved; these will provide an overall representation of the collection and may prevent designs from being lost.

Sketches can be further developed by over-drawing on your original images to make improvements that may not have been obvious to you at the start of the process. Some of your designs may prove to be inappropriate for the collection, and so should be carefully labelled and archived as potential sources of inspiration for the next season or trend. Remember: mistakes often lead to other ideas!

Development work

The meaning of development work is to take an initial design and change the proportion, size, detail or features of it, little by little, in order to give some added dimension to the accessory. Design development improves a designer's ability to mix and match through trial and error in order to create an innovative accessory. Colours, styles, shapes and textures can be explored in different combinations and developed to correspond to the designer's signature look. At this stage, the designs should be assessed for suitability and to ensure that they meet the purpose and expectations of the design brief. As not all designs will be made into prototypes or put into production, careful selection of the strongest designs will be necessary.

Creative product development

8

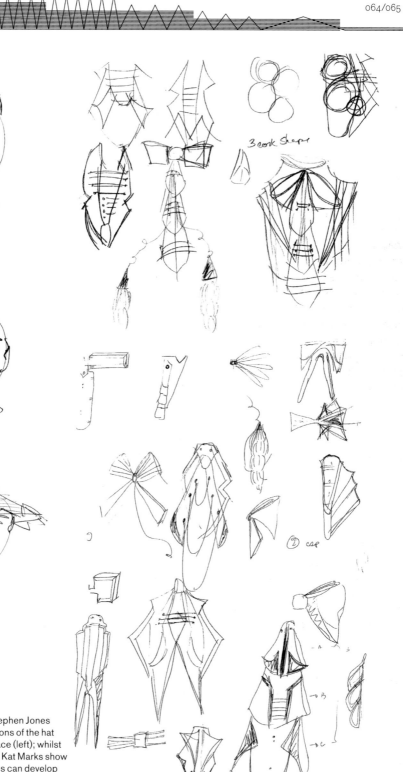

3 cork shape

2 cap

8. Sketches by Stephen Jones show the proportions of the hat in relation to the face (left); whilst quick sketches by Kat Marks show how simple shapes can develop into contemporary jewellery pieces (right).

There are two main types of presentation techniques that can be treated separately or in combination. Design work presented in a creative format includes hand and computer illustrations, and specifications demonstrate the technical format. Commercial designs have a clear link to the intended target customer.

Most presentations require carefully selected imagery, including photographs, designs and sketches, as well as fabric and trims to emphasize your intentions, and text such as titles and descriptions. These should reflect the style of the accessories collection as well as the designer's personality. There are many methods of presentation, such as building layers creatively to convey a narrative or through the creation of a formulaic grid using computer-aided design, hand drawing or a combination of both to give added depth to the presentation. Whilst drawing skills must be developed, computer-aided design is today the tool of choice most widely used in the accessories industry.

10

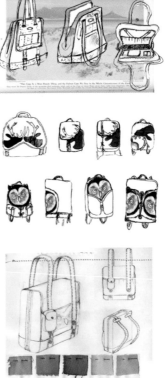

9

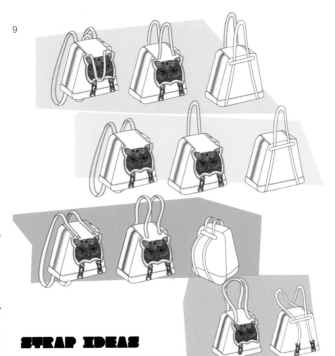

STRAP IDEAS

9. Design specification demonstrating functions, style and colour by Hattie Hignell.

10. A series of hand drawings by Hattie Hignell demonstrates traditional presentation techniques to clearly show how the bag design functions and develops.

Creative product development

Computer-aided design (CAD)

Sophisticated computer technology and software enables designers to create illustrations and technical drawings easily and in very little time. Adobe Creative Suite is the most popular design package used in the industry. Adobe Photoshop, a pixel-based program, is mainly used for image editing, such as airbrushing photographs. A useful program to improve images, the main disadvantage of Photoshop is the decrease in quality when resizing images to a larger size, although this can be simply overcome by using original high-resolution images. The vector-based program Adobe Illustrator uses lines and curves, and images that have been scaled using the software do not lose quality. The two programs can be used together and designers are increasingly versatile in their abilities to use both.

Adobe InDesign can create layouts or most projects that require publication. Pages and portfolio layouts can be easily produced with the use of a template, which can be quicker and easier to modify once it has been created. This program gives designers the ability to communicate visually through many channels including design, production and manufacturing. Any computer software will take time to learn and fully utilize, but the results can make designing accessories in any discipline much more efficient.

Specifications

The function of the working sketch is to inform the reader of the accessory's shape, style features, size, fabric and trimmings. The sketch is not a stylized drawing but a realistic one that clearly shows the entire seam and construction lines, along with all the other style features in fine detail. Front and back views are the minimum requirements; however, close-up drawings are required to clearly illustrate complicated detailing, or style details that are not readily apparent in the sketch. On the specifications, include written descriptions of the accessory, including relevant design details and specific manufacturing requirements. Finally, attach samples of fabric, interfacing, lining and trimmings to the sketch.

11

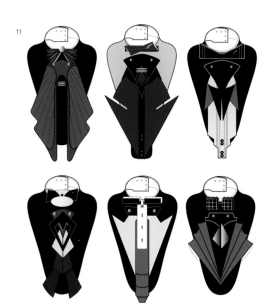

11. Complete designs showing exact colour scheme by Kat Marks.

Idea generation > **Presentation techniques** > Market levels

Accessories are continually developed to improve the final outcome and throughout the design process, key products will emerge. It is important to identify these key products and to determine their appropriate place within the existing market. These accessories will then form the main part of the collection used for advertising and display on catwalk shows, either as standalone pieces that others can derive from or as one-of-a-kind showcase pieces. Key products have the ability to entice customers and generate publicity because of their unique qualities, and may remain highly influential for many years.

12. A dramatic use of feathers in a flamboyant headdress from Jean Paul Gaultier's Haute Couture Spring/Summer 2010 collection.

13. Oversize buckles and tribal influences are woven into the fabric of this clutch bag from Burberry Prorsum's Spring/Summer 2012 collection.

14. Gold leather bandage-like straps wrap around the heavy wedge heel by Diesel Black Gold for their Spring/Summer 2012 collection.

12

13

14

The three market levels

For many years, the high-end level of the accessories market has dominated both trends and designs. Haute couture shows in Paris and the other fashion capitals continue to show handmade accessories in biannual collections; established brands, such as Hermès, continue to manufacture bags in the finest leathers while Harry Winston constructs jewellery with top-quality gemstones, for instance. This type of design and intricate work reflects the pricing of the accessory.

There are three main market levels to consider when designing a commercial collection:

- The high-end is regarded as the market leader and is expected to set the pace of the industry, leading the way in design, styles and trends.

- The mid-level responds quickly to changes when trends trickle down to the mass market.

- The low-end is usually on trend but uses lower-quality materials to create the accessories. However, this market level is considered to be the value sector and it continues to grow quickly on a global scale.

Well-known designers have transcended each level to create accessories across all areas and have learnt to use their status to design for the lucrative lower-end markets.

Ready-to-wear is by far the largest market in the accessories industry. Accessories are created in mass quantities to exact specifications, generally using less expensive materials and simpler processes. This part of the industry exists in all three market levels and relies on speed to ensure that products reach the retail stores in time.

When designing a range, there are three layers to consider: the good, better and best range. The three-layered approach ensures differentiation between the accessories and demonstrates the value in a range. After identifying the key products, a range is developed to fulfil commercial responsibilities. Commercial ranges require a wide but coherent selection of accessories. Initial stages will involve planning the number of lines within a collection.

The industry has four main product classifications. Staple products are considered 'classics' and products within the range rarely change. Changes in accessory designs steadily increase for semi-styled and styled products. The final classification is called 'fashion', because the styles change regularly or are rejected entirely after a relatively short time. A range can be organized by several methods, including the colour of the accessories and their size, by using the average as a guide to the number of accessories to produce.

Product lines

There are two main product lines:

– product-line length refers to how many styles there are in a range;

– product-line depth indicates how many variations there will be within one style.

15–16. Combining functional components that take into consideration the comfort of the wearer, these line sheets by student Elin Melin show the main styles and key components that feature within her range of boot designs.

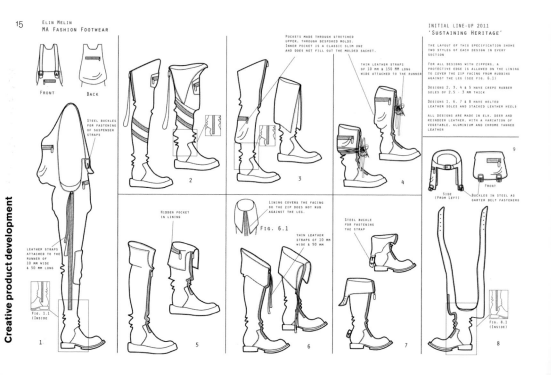

ELIN MELIN
MA FASHION FOOTWEAR

INITIAL LINE-UP 2011
'SUSTAINING HERITAGE'

Bag

Bag collections are vast and continue to grow. Exclusive ranges have a very small amount produced because of the complexity of the design or the rarity of the materials used. Many broad commercial ranges feature bags from all product classifications.

Jewellery

Jewellery ranges are reliant on the budget available for raw materials. Precious metals and gemstones are expensive and require large investments to purchase, therefore the range needs careful planning. Cheaper materials are used for commercial ranges.

Footwear

With a high turnover of shoes within a season, commercial footwear ranges can be very large because of the combination of styles and sizes. Classic ranges have longevity; however, fashion ranges have a shorter life span because shoes will have been designed for a specific trend.

Millinery

Ranges for hats and caps from high-end brands can be small due to the intricate work required. Size is an important issue when creating hats; however, standard sizes can be stretched using a hat stretcher. Commercial millinery has larger ranges in a broader selection of sizes and colours.

16

ELIN MELIN
MA FASHION FOOTWEAR

INITIAL LINE-UP 2011
'SUSTAINING HERITAGE'

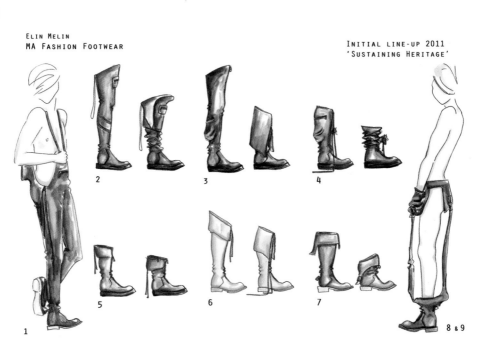

2
3
4
5
6
7
1
8 & 9

Market levels > **Developing a range** > Industry perspective

An influential designer with work that has been showcased in books and exhibited in museums, as well as appearing on numerous catwalk shows, Scott Wilson has an exceptional eye for fine detail and hand finishing that has been widely critically acclaimed. His career has involved designing accessories for Thierry Mugler, Hussein Chalayan, Julien Macdonald and Givenchy Couture. Some of Scott's most recognizable pieces are those he is regularly commissioned to create, such as the one-of-a-kind pieces for his celebrity clients, who include Nicole Kidman, Kylie Minogue and Madonna.

Why did you decide to enter the accessories industry and how did it happen?

I have always been fascinated with the ability to wear something on the body other than clothing, as well as being drawn to three-dimensional objects. During my four years studying BA Jewellery Design at Middlesex University in London, an internship in year three led me to Showroom Seven in New York, a fashion and accessories showroom, which incorporates the jewellery brand Erickson Beamon. Working there, as well as later working for Erickson Beamon co-founder Vicki Sarge, helped me to comprehend fashion jewellery in a way that I had not previously considered, having come from a more contemporary jewellery background. I then moved on to the Royal College of Art in London, where I completed a Masters in Womenswear and Millinery, which helped me to formulate a multitude of new ideas and set a more distinctly different pathway for my design career.

Where do you start when sourcing inspiration?

Inspiration for me can be found in a myriad of ways; from the most mundane things to the most exciting. As a creative individual who thinks of himself as a problem solver, I am always looking around to see how things are made, how they are constructed and how materials are positioned next to each other, for example. What greatly influences me is making processes, as well as forms, shapes and volumes that fascinate me.

17–20. Scott Wilson combines different polishing techniques to achieve a balance of rough and smooth when creating his jewellery. This combination of elements highlights the many facets and highly reflective surfaces of the pieces.

18

19

20

What is your design process?

I work on a variety of design projects, and equally my design processes also differ accordingly, especially when collaborating with fashion brands. Generally, I would start with thorough research aimed towards realizing a direction as to what materials are best suited for the purposes of the project, as well as towards determining the shape and the core forms, which are required to create the overall outcome.

How do you source your components and materials and why do you use them most?

My initial brief helps to determine whether I will use ready-made components or whether I will make those components or the whole piece from scratch. No material is out of bounds in terms of being able to be used; this of course depends on the criteria of the initial brief. Metal is incredibly versatile, for example, and can be formed into almost anything utilizing a variety of techniques. Acrylic is also another of my favourite materials, which I've used extensively over the years.

How do you develop your range every season?

Life doesn't stand still: neither does what inspires us. Being aware of trends, of what people are wearing, as well as having a grasp of what the future trends are likely to be, is important. Very often, my starting point for a collection will be one specific piece that creates the central axis for the group, which I then design the rest of the range from.

Scott Wilson

What aspect of your work is most recognizable?

Statement pieces that are bold, incorporating modern shapes, or that present an unexpected juxtaposition of materials, which are often almost object-like in form. My work clearly references 1970s modern design and architecture, infused with the spirit of art deco.

What inspires you when you collaborate with other designers?

I've collaborated on more than 70 catwalk shows with a variety of designers as well as other collaborations ranging from Toni & Guy to Lindt Chocolate and Repetto-Paris shoes. Each collaboration is different; each relationship you form with a specific brand influences your decision-making as to how and what you design. Being able to work with a specific brand's aesthetic while blending in your own signature has endless possibilities that one may not otherwise be able to develop within your own collection.

What can you learn from specially commissioned pieces?

Specially commissioned pieces can come in a myriad of forms; they can be time-sensitive, financially pressured, complex on many levels, often something you've not designed or made before. For example, the award that we recently designed and made for Zaha Hadid, the Jane Drew Prize for Hadid's contribution to women in architecture, was the first award I've ever designed. The objective of special commissions is to satisfy not only yourself but someone else as well. What better way is there for a designer to test their skills?

Why are accessories an important feature in a fashion collection?

For me, an accessory can be anything beyond the clothing, which allows for endless possibilities and interpretations of the garments. The accessories themselves can deviate from being über-minimalist or super extravagant, as well as all the limitless interceptions of everything in between. I believe accessories can add richness to a collection, much like a full stop does to a sentence.

What can a new designer learn from your journey in accessories design?

Without stating all the clichés, I've always strived to be happy with what I design and what I make. I've preserved my passion to experiment and create and have done so without fear of getting it wrong. Mistakes can be a valuable learning process, just as much as can getting it right.

21. Scott Wilson effectively unites contrasting colour combinations in these complex pieces that utilize large rings and chains mixed with plaited twists of metal.

Creative product development

21

The aim of building a portfolio is to demonstrate the skill, knowledge and best work of a designer. A portfolio should not be static or work as an archive, but should instead function as a showcase that truly reflects the designer's personality. As your skills develop, the work presented should focus on your strengths in your chosen field: bags, footwear, millinery or jewellery.

New designers are advised to show a full range of accessories in their portfolios; however, as your career progresses, a confident designer will come to possess a signature style. Designers have to create a flexible portfolio to meet many needs, including: presenting to potential employers; meeting with individual clients; displaying past work; and updating the portfolio on a regular basis to showcase developing skills in your chosen area.

Creating your portfolio electronically

Designers regularly work with computer technology to create a portfolio. The work can be reproduced by photocopying, scanning and photographing. Designing portfolio layouts in a publishing programme allows them to be easily formatted electronically, and ready to be shared by email, either as a PDF or JPEG document or uploaded onto a website.

22

23

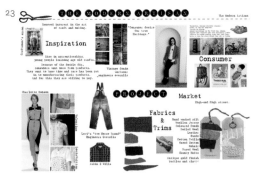

22–24. Examples of professional portfolios by Heather Stable, which show the design process from initial research on a moodboard through to a line sheet showing design development ideas. One of the final pieces is also shown (left).

Creative product development

24

Shirred jersey dress bodice with woven skirt and button stand. Vintage button fastening.

Waxed cotton and wool blazer with false waistcoat fastening and leather straps at wrist.

Suede Pinafore dress with buckle & button fastening detail.

Leather harness with leather pockets and antique brass buckles.

Striped cotton, smocked shirt with suede coallr & side cowl details.

The Modern Artisan

Organization and contents

What goes into the portfolio depends on the purpose it's required for; for instance, whether you're seeking your first job, or showing it to a potential client or manufacturer. It is crucial that you organize your work so that it shows off a range of skills. A newer designer will have examples of work that show the design process.

Strong inspirational images from a sketchbook can be colour-photocopied for inclusion in the portfolio, along with design sheets, flat technical drawings, final designs and photographs of completed accessories. Accompanying text to explain the work is always helpful and will be a useful fallback if you become lost for words in your meeting!

Format

The format in which you present your work depends on the type of portfolio that you would like to build; therefore, selecting the correct case, format and size is crucial. If the work is heavily reliant on tactile pieces, an archive box will prove a better option. Consider the size of the portfolio, too, as many clients, manufacturers and potential employers have limited available space. The traditional format of a ring binder with plastic sleeves gives a professional look and ensures that the work is clean and clear, which is particularly effective when presenting commercial work. The work in your portfolio should be of a consistent standard, so always edit out any work that is unsuitable or rework weak areas. To determine the pace of the portfolio, ensure that you place work that has the strongest impact at the start and end of the presentation.

Design task 2:

Single board development

New designers will accumulate work from many different areas during their time of study and practice. Careful editing is therefore an essential skill to master, requiring a confident designer to judge the best, essential and most effective work. Presenting work that is uncluttered will communicate your message clearly to the intended audience.

Objective and learning outcome

For this activity, you will use existing work to create a single board that shows the design process of an accessory.

Design task

Begin by collecting work from a variety of areas including: inspirational visuals; design development; sketches and design illustrations; final designs; and technical specifications. Edit the visuals to include only the essential images associated with the selected accessory, deciding on the main focal objective of the board, such as design development or technical specifications.

Divide the single board into a grid pattern – symmetrical areas bring consistency to inconsistent sizes and shapes. Place the work into a logical grid pattern with the selected objective as the main focal point, finally adding a title and a short description of the work. Expand on existing work by altering the designs and specifications to suit a different market area. For example, high-end and exclusive accessory designs are redesigned for the mass-market customer and conversely mid-market trends may be redesigned for designer labels.

Design a new range for the market by using only two design elements and features from the original accessory. Create designs to fit into the good, better and best categories. Present the designs clearly, including a short description, on a single board.

HATTIE HIGNELL

Too much, too young? Retai selling over-sexualised cloth

Creative product development

A Feral Collection

"This Cape Is a Most Stately Thing, and the Fairest Cape We Saw in the Whole Circumference of the Earth"

You Can Pick Your Own "Queen Coffee" from This Line-up of Athletic Beauties at São Paulo

Girl Scout Series

25. Moodboard showing inspirational images for Hattie Hignell's Feral Collection.

26

Stephen Jones

Why did you decide to join this dynamic industry?

It was not really an active decision: I merged into it. I did not start out with great ambition but, somehow, millinery chose me; that is how I always feel about it, that it was the right thing to do and it was something I loved. I studied fashion at Central Saint Martin's College of Art and Design in London but wasn't good at sewing. I became an intern at a couture house to improve my sewing in the tailoring workroom, which was next to the millinery workroom – and that's how this started. I've always loved making things, from model aeroplanes to toys, and millinery is similar; dressmaking or tailoring is draped around a body.

What inspires you most in millinery?

The first thing that attracted me to it was the people, who are all a little crazy and real characters. People arrive in millinery via strange routes so you tend to encounter people from very different backgrounds and from all around the world, which is fascinating. It's great that people can travel to this country [the UK] and express themselves. Secondly, there's the spontaneity of millinery. You can pick up a ball of tissue paper and put it on somebody's head and it becomes a hat, if you want it to be. There is something very dynamic about hats.

Where do your ideas originate?

When I start to design a collection, it all comes from the concept. There must be a concept of something – whether it is fourteenth century or Scottish or modern – literally from every waking moment. A recent collection is called Chinoiserie-on-Sea, which was inspired by a trip to Brighton, UK. I love the fact that Brighton is a place which combines the seaside and all the seaside metaphors with the chinoiserie of the Royal Pavilion. I love the misunderstanding that Westerners had of the Orient, which to most was everything east of the English Channel or the North Sea! I love small details. Inspiration can come from books, paintings, travelling and anything. I always make sure that I am open to everything. I start off with something and then start to build the world around it. In parallel, I research fabric at manufacturers all over the world, especially in Italy and Japan. That's how I start a collection.

Why is accessory design different from clothing design?

I have found people that go into millinery because they cannot draw well, because they work more in the three-dimensional, such as jewellers or bag makers or shoemakers. Dress designers on the other hand work a lot with two-dimensional design, so they have to be good at drawing. Fashion is about blocking things out, but millinery works the other way round. What I love is having the means to a variety of expression. But as a rule, people are becoming more and more categorized – if you look at what people were able to do 20 or 30 years ago, it was more expressive than what people can do now; what people wear on the street today is much less extravagant than in former times. There are also standards and rules to clothing design that do not exist in millinery.

27

A style-blazer from his very first days in London, Stephen Jones is the foremost creative force in millinery, with a legion of loyal followers including Kylie Minogue, Beyoncé Knowles and Dita Von Teese, who truly appreciate this master of idiosyncratic design. His hats have been described as modern, refined and whimsical. Stephen manages to maximize the possibilities of materials to create exquisitely crafted designs – turning fantasy into reality.

26–27. Stephen Jones uses bold shapes and colours for his whimsical designs that show off his astounding skill at proportioning a hat for a face. Jones's contemporary hats boast a master's knowledge of millinery at its very best.

Stephen Jones

How do you work on your shapes?

After the initial designs, we make toiles in the three-dimensional form using a block. We also have a model to try out the shapes in the workroom. There are usually lots of alterations which need making, which is why it's always important to get someone to try the toile on. You may have an idea of what the piece should look like, but ultimately you have to see the design on a person: the model can also bring something more to the design.

What materials do you use and why?

I use all sorts of materials, from plastic to microfibres to ones that light up. I use good-quality classics because they are tried and tested, such as white cotton and black velvet. The big difference between hats and clothing is that millinery can utilize fabrics that are not washable. Fabrics can be worked on with solutions and sculpted, before being worked up directly into a form.

What aspect of your work do you think is most recognizable?

The most recognizable aspects are my lightness of touch and sense of humour, which shows optimism. A lot of millinery has no bearing on reality because it wants to entertain those who try the hats on.

What inspires you when collaborating with other designers?

Working with other people is fascinating; when collaborating, seeing inside the minds of others in terms of how they work and finding out what makes them tick is great. I am extremely privileged to work with the best and there is always a lesson to be learnt from how they do things.

What can you learn from working with private clients?

Working with private clients is not so different; they are ordering a hat that is special and this is what they themselves want to be. You have to listen to them and what they want because this is why they have come to you. However, they are often also happy to be led because you're the expert after all!

Why will millinery continue to be an important accessory in the future?

Unlike clothing, people rarely throw hats away. People are very involved with their hats, which are highly personal yet also public. Other accessories you can put aside but you wear a hat on a part of your body that is highly visible. It influences how you present yourself, whether at a formal event or other occasion.

What are the important lessons a new designer can learn from your experience in the industry?

Perseverance. This will come in handy when you are unpicking at 5am – but you should have fun along the way. With millinery, you must begin by making hats for real people – do it for the people that surround you and they will always appreciate that. Designing for the hypothetical person is not always practical and if real people love your work then you have been successful. Also, you have to remember that to be successful you cannot do it all by yourself. What I do takes a whole movement of people to get right. Honestly loving what you do will always make people follow you.

28. The details and features on Stephen Jones's hats display the milliner's boundless creativity, which inspires his contemporaries and wearers alike.

28

3

The 1940s look of structured leather handbags with heavy handles and contrasting cut-outs from behind the scenes at Marni's Autumn/Winter 2012–13 fashion show.

All accessories entail different methods of construction and designing an accessory often involves building on the years of skills and knowledge which already exist. For example, Europe – notably France, the UK and Italy – has been creating exceptional accessories with globally recognized craftsmanship for centuries; construction techniques have typically been passed from generation to generation, providing a foundation for a brand's signature style.

Highly original accessories can only come about by drawing on this strong tradition of innovation and by incorporating tried-and-tested techniques to create beautiful pieces. Today, designers utilize traditional techniques with new technologies to build upon this existing knowledge, further preserving innovative construction techniques for the future. Careful archiving has also enabled new generations of designers to learn about the heritage of brands from the libraries of accessories created.

1–2. By using traditional methods of manufacturing handed down over the generations, the heritage of world-renowned eyewear designer Oliver Goldsmith is continued through his great granddaughter Claire Goldsmith's contemporary take on classic spectacle frame designs.

1

Some companies have amassed huge collections of tools over the years that they have been trading, which often come to be handed down over each generation. As such, these tools become an invaluable resource, which support a company's growing knowledge and skill in their specialism.

This chapter thus begins with an introductory description of the essential tools that a designer will require for bag making, footwear manufacture, jewellery construction and millinery production, as a designer will require and acquire many tools over the course of their career. The tools introduced here are those which you will need to learn about in order for you to get started with constructing accessories.

Accessories are formed into shapes from mainly flat materials and learning about these basic techniques is important to develop a foundation for understanding more advanced techniques. The best lessons can be learned from understanding the basic principles and simultaneously watching and learning from more experienced practitioners.

Experimentation will then enable you to gain confidence in their practice and thereby continually improve. But first, you must learn the fundamental rules and then later, as confidence grows, you must learn how to break them!

There are many construction methods that arrive at the same outcome and this chapter aims to offer a snapshot of the many available to accessories designers.

2

Bags

Creating a bag is akin to making many other fashion products, including clothing, jewellery and other accessories. The design of a bag can be complicated – with many attachments or hardware, for instance – or it can be very simple. The tools for manufacturing bags are basic; however, they all have the ability to help the designer to construct beautiful accessories. Traditional techniques using these tools are continually explored by designers alongside the use of innovative new technologies.

3. Inside his workshop, Lee Mattocks presents his completed bag in pristine white leather.

Foundation materials

Leather
A wide range of leathers are available, from the most common – cowhide – to the more exotic, such as alligator. Always check the provenance of the leather to ensure that no endangered species are mistakenly used.

Fabric
The fabric used for bags is usually strong and thick enough to withstand the carrying of heavy objects.

Canvas
A range of thicknesses is available, in both natural and synthetic fibres, to support and retain the shape of leather or fabric.

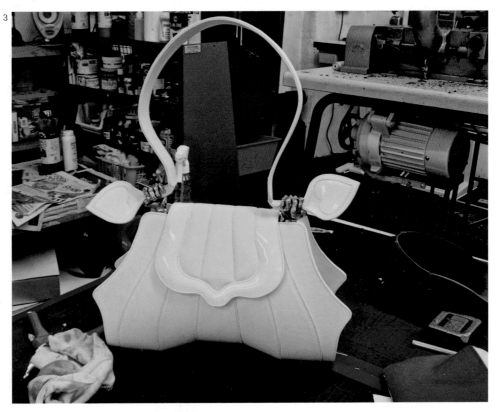

3

Construction tools

Awl
This tool is used for making both discreet marks and larger holes.

Pattern paper and card
Drafting patterns is a lengthy process and requires the use of pattern paper and card to accurately trace the pattern pieces onto leather or fabric.

Frames
A wide selection of frames is available in different shapes and sizes to suit the type of bag required.

Rings
Rings, available in many shapes, are very strong to hold the strap and withstand heavy-duty wear and tear.

Hole punch
A hole punch with various sizes is an excellent tool for making uniform holes.

Bag fastenings
Numerous types of fasteners are available for specific bags or functions, including zips, toggles and clasps.

Wooden mallet
A mallet can be used for all types of job, including fixing hardware onto the bag or beating open seams for a flat finish.

Sewing machine
Sewing machines must be robust enough to handle both thick fabrics and hard leather. Machine part components should be checked regularly.

Pliers
Used for bending metal pieces, such as rings, or for fixing hardware onto the bag.

Arnoldo][Battois

4. Silvano Arnoldo and Massimiliano Battois.

Silvano Arnoldo and Massimiliano Battois are the design duo behind Arnoldo][Battois, a contemporary accessories company with a focus on handbags with touches of intricate details and modern finishing techniques. Their professional training was born from haute couture and prêt-a-porter as designers for major brands – Mila Schön, Pierre Cardin and Laura Biagiotti. The discovery of accessories came later, in collaboration with Roberta di Camerino.

How did you begin your journey in this dynamic industry?

We met at Venice International University in the Faculty of Architecture and one day, while we were simply sitting at our desks in class, we discovered a strong common desire for fashion. So we started training and working in the realm of design, arriving in Milan to become part of Mila Schön's haute couture staff. That was our formative experience in fashion, which was followed by further work experience at the Marzotto Group, Scherrer, Cardin, Laura Biagiotti and René Caovilla. These roles then flowed naturally into a long collaboration with Roberta di Camerino, which was fundamental for our creative growth and the discovery of a new shared passion: handbag design.

What made you decide to establish your own label?

We created our brand Arnoldo][Battois in 2010 after we were confronted with the question, 'What next?'. We wanted to gain further recognition and a higher profile, but realized that we could not achieve this by ourselves. We were then one of three finalists in the accessories category of a competition, which made us resume our work with added confidence. In September 2010, we showed our Spring/Summer 2011 collection during Milan Fashion Week, at an event organized by *Vogue Italy* and *Vogue USA* in Palazzo Morando, in the presence of Franca Sozzani, Anna Wintour and some of the most important names in the fashion industry.

Where does your inspiration originate? How do you work on your shapes?

Our sources of inspiration for our work come from very different worlds, but it is from their meeting points that ideas are born. Every eye-catching detail and nuance can re-emerge in new combinations. Also, elements of the natural world and architecture constantly influence the collections, shapes, colours and textures.

What is the most important feature in your collections?

The element that is found in all of our collections is our link with Venice. We were born, then brought together with Roberta di Camerino, in this amazing city. Despite our different experiences in other Italian and foreign cities, we chose to create our collection and establish Arnoldo][Battois in Venice because of our strong bond with this city that seems suspended in time. Venice is a place of historical sedimentation and fertilization of culture, where the glories of the *Serenissima*, the travels of Marco Polo and the lives of intellectuals and artists of the past continues to feed into contemporary culture.

5–6. Soft leather handbags by Arnoldo][Battois, which use soft folds, gathers and clever seaming to create unique contours.

7–8. The intense colours used for these bags highlight the soft folds of the distinctively shaped bags.

Arnoldo][Battois

What is your design process?

The element that unites us is the conception of the creative act as an 'architectural' complex, with structures and rules to be respected: we always seek coherence between form and content. Our differences are very successful aspects of every project; the creative clash of ideas goes towards what makes us unique and special, and finally results in excellence. The mood of the collection and processing of the main contents, including the choice of materials and colours, is always the result of extensive discussion and debate. The issues highlighted are processed, discussed and summarized in the final choices for the collection.

How do you source your materials?

The Arnoldo][Battois collections are made entirely in Italy, in the Riviera del Brenta (Venice) where the knowledge of centuries-old tradition enables us to create excellent quality and unique pieces. The materials we use are varied, but all are produced and processed in Italy, from soft plongé nappa barrel with natural dyes to aniline calf and waxed python. Even in the interior linings, we seek to bring exclusivity through our use of duchesse satin.

What details inspire your collections?

Our philosophy is to work on details and search for innovative solutions, such as through manual processes that allow you to rediscover the essence of traditional Italian products. Venice is a continuing source of fascination for new details including lizards, crabs and brass elephants: for example, the old Venetian doors in our special or unusual closures; the Arsenal, the heart of Venice, provides inspiration for handles and details; the tops of ships might become soft nappa plots for ergonomic handles.

What essential elements must an accessories designer consider?

Objects in flux and change must adapt to different situations, especially handbags, which are typically designed to be worn independently of the proportions and dynamics of the body. However, we feel that these accessories should instead exploit the movement of the body, using combinations of different materials, and so define themselves.

9

10

Construction techniques

What is the future development of Arnoldo][Battois?

While we are consolidating the collection of bags for Arnoldo][Battois, we have a new project underway to build a ready-to-wear collection that reflects and transforms the features of our accessories. The clothing will be designed as accessories, taking inspiration from the essential structures that define and surround the human figure.

9–10. Arnoldo][Battois uses a juxtaposition of hard and soft in these bags with heavy metal features, which clamp tightly onto the supple leather.

11–12. Neon piping cleverly incorporated into the seams glows against the pastel leather used to create these handbags.

13–14. Perspex and laser cutting reinterprets an antique design, boldly contrasting against the teal-coloured leather.

11

13

12

14

Footwear

Tools for making footwear are generally very strong and robust. Large tools are used for making finely detailed shoes, ranging from the most important tool, the 'last', to the smallest nails that permanently hold the components of the shoe together. New technological developments have further expanded the equipment available for manufacturing footwear.

This introduction details the main tools required for constructing shoes; however, many more are available to the highly skilled designer and shoemaker.

Last

The last is a very important tool for constructing footwear and is a shoemaker's model for shaping or repairing a shoe or boot. A last is required for different shapes and sizes, for the left and right foot, for different toecap shapes and heel heights for each shoe, with each last made for a single specific shoe. Lasts are traditionally made in wood, although plastic lasts are becoming very popular as these can be made up much faster and production costs are significantly lower.

Foundation materials

Leather
The most important material used in the footwear industry, from the most common – cowhide – to the most expensive – crocodile and kid leather.

Fabric
Shoes are made in all types of fabrics for a variety of functions, including the purely decorative. Highly innovative materials encompassing new technological advances are designed to create enhanced comfort and breathability in sports shoes.

Interlining
Synthetic and natural interlining provides comfort and warmth to all types of footwear, including work boots and sports shoes.

Canvas
Synthetic and natural canvas is used for backing fabric and leather to retain the shape of the shoe.

15

15. A wooden shoe last forms the basis of most shoemaking.

Construction tools

Lasting pliers
Lasting pliers are used for pulling leather tightly across the last for a close fit, and for stretching areas to prevent buckling and to create a smooth finish.

Shoe hammer
A small metal hammer used for a range of jobs, including hammering nails, attaching the heel to the sole, and adhering cemented parts together.

Leather-working mallet
A leather mallet is designed to avoid marking and damaging the material's surface, and is utilized for a variety of roles, such as flattening and creating sharp folds.

Nails
Available in a wide selection for holding pieces together both temporarily and permanently.

Adhesives
A range of adhesives for permanently holding pieces together is available, including cement for leather and glue for synthetic materials.

Rotary cutter
A sharp rotary cutter can cut thick pieces of leather and fabric, but must be used in conjunction with a self-healing mat to avoid damaging surfaces.

Jewellery

Jewellery requires the most tools of all the accessories discussed in this book. Tools are designed to save time and effort; however, a collection is amassed over a number of years as a designer's skills grow. Construction tools can be basic but also expensive (according to their quality), although most tools will last for a long time if they are well looked after.

It is crucial that the workstation has good lighting and a high bench to avoid injury; therefore, setting up a work area and organizing the work equipment is vital to jewellery making.

Further useful equipment

Ring mandrel
A steel cone that tapers to a point, used for making rings circular.

Doming punches
In conjunction with a doming block, punches are available in boxwood or steel for making domes. They must be kept smooth and clean to give a perfect finish because any damage will transfer directly onto the piece of jewellery being worked on.

Pickling solution
Sulphuric acid is used for removing impurities from jewellery, such as stains, because it is very corrosive. Take caution: adding water to acid creates a dangerous reaction. Always, always add acid to water!

Construction tools

Bench peg and anvil
A bench peg and anvil is used for steadying pieces of jewellery during the construction process.

Adjustable saw and blades
A frame must be large enough to manoeuvre around pieces of work and a selection of blades will be required for different types of work, including very fine blades for intricate pieces.

Drill
Both electric and non-electric drills require very little pressure to operate. Drill bits are required to cut holes in various sizes in different materials.

Screwdriver
A selection of screwdrivers is available in different sizes.

Metal hammer
For shaping and flattening metal; also used for smoothing.

Drill bits
A selection of drill bits is available depending on the size required. The twist drill bit is the most common; these rotate clockwise to cut a hole.

Snips
This tool is used for cutting larger sheets of metal.

Wooden mallet
Used to lengthen by stretching, thinning out and smoothing metals; a mallet is also used for gently tapping pieces together without marking the materials.

File
These are available in a range of sizes and fineness for different types of work.

Torch
Used to heat metals and other materials, and used for soldering.

Industry perspective > **Essential tools of the trade** > Exploring construction techniques

Millinery

16

The tools used for millinery vary greatly, ranging from large wooden blocks to very fine needles. Depending on the type of hat or cap design, some tools are more important than others. New millinery techniques have expanded the types of tools used, as designers continue to experiment with new materials. This introduction includes the main construction tools and foundation materials that a new designer is likely to encounter; however, there are many more available for different types of techniques, designs and features that you might like to research further yourself.

Foundation materials

Foundation fabric and materials
The fabrics used for millinery were traditionally felt and straw, but now include a wide variety of other materials, including plastics and lightweight metals.

Buckram
Available in a range of looser or tighter weaves, the material is coated in different amounts of starch for flexibility. The material is pliable when wet but stiff when dry.

Net
Heat and steam from an iron softens the net, which is blocked over hat blocks so that it retains its shape when dry.

Elastic
Wide and narrow varieties are used to hold different areas securely.

Tape
Bias tape covers exposed edges and wires, neatening them for comfort and safety.

16. A huge collection of wooden hat blocks and a wealth of history are kept inside Stephen Jones's millinery studio.

Construction techniques

Construction tools

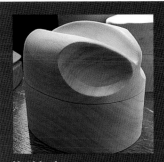

Hat blocks
The heavy blocks are created in wood in different sizes and shapes in relation to the type and style of hat or cap, with separate matching blocks for brims if required.

Scissors
Available in a variety of sizes and designs for specific roles, including fabric shears, paper and card, and small trimming and embroidery scissors.

Millinery wire
Available in a range of thicknesses, the wire is covered in cotton thread and is used for firm brim edges or to hold areas and features in place.

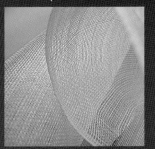

Linings
A soft and breathable fabric that is used to hide raw edges and neaten the interior of a hat.

Sewing machines
Good starter machines offer the flexibility of a range of stitches for general domestic use: industrial machinery is used in factories for commercial production.

Stiffeners
To give body and shape to fabric, stiffeners are a type of varnish that can be applied by brush or spray.

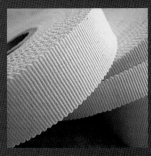

Petersham ribbon
The ribbon can be stretched and shrunk with heat from an iron to fit curved and brim edges.

Needles
A variety of hand-sewing needles are used for specific purposes, ranging from very fine, long or curved.

Bags

Bags can be simple and can be made with a single pattern piece; or they may be very complex, consisting of many smaller pieces. Construction begins by selecting suitable essential hardware or ornamental components for the piece.

The bag can firstly be made in card or felt in order for the designer to judge the shape, structure and size of the bag. The pattern size and placement may be limited by the size of the leather and must be thought through at the early stages of pattern making.

Pattern making

Establish the size of the bag on pattern paper by working out the dimensions using a ruler and set square. A series of basic blocks from which many styles are adapted can be made in heavy-duty card or plastic, although each style of bag will have its own unique set of patterns. Add seam allowances along the edges of the patterns, being careful to note that some areas, such as corners, will require a smaller allowance to reduce bulk. However, fabric that easily frays along the edges will require a much larger seam allowance.

Cutting

Cutting requires skill. Mark the pattern pieces on the leather or fabric with chalk, so ensuring precision. Use very sharp fabric shears to cut the marked pattern pieces or use rotary cutters for more flexibility, especially for cutting skins precisely – mistakes can be very costly! Commercial production will require a bandsaw to cut through many layers of fabric at once, requiring exceptional skill to operate the machinery. This method of cutting is imprecise and only useful for larger pattern pieces. Snip tiny notches within the seam allowance to match pieces together when assembling the bag.

17

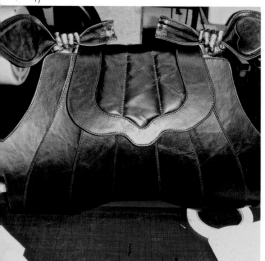

18

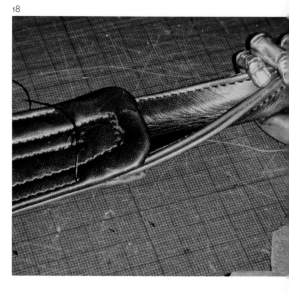

Assembling

The construction process begins with careful planning of the sequence of operations, whether a bag is to be assembled completely by hand or by machine on an assembly line for commercial bags. Experienced machinists can produce bags quickly, but a new designer will usually make small batches.

The most important thing at this stage is to have the frame and other hardware for difficult-to-reach areas attached. Any frame that may need building, especially for hard-sided bags, will need to be completed and to have the leather attached using adhesives (and possibly tacking nails) to hold it securely in place. Any filler being used will also need to be inserted at this stage, for example to create a quilting effect. Insert any stiffening materials, such as canvas, to hold the shape of the bag.

Stitching

For making bags by machine, a simple lockstitch machine can perform most basic tasks provided it is capable of sewing leather, can hold the correct needle for doing so, and has a Teflon®-coated foot or walking foot to prevent the leather from sticking and thick material from dragging.

Stitching bags by hand is a lengthy process. Small holes are pre-made at precise intervals using the saddle stitch, a popular technique for high-quality bags, which involves two needles being passed back and forth through the holes. This technique gives an even finish because the stitch line is unbroken on both sides. Beeswax is used to strengthen the thread and avoid tangles. Practising using scrap pieces of leather or fabric will ensure that the correct tension has been achieved prior to completing the final product.

17. Shown here is the prototype that was made to check proportion and silhouette for the Lee Mattocks bag previously shown on page 88.

18–20. Leather sampler Katie Harding puts the finishing touches on the final handbag by Lee Mattocks.

19

20

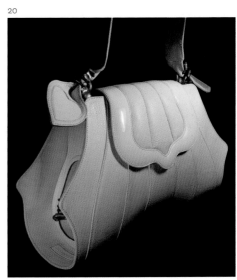

Essential tools of the trade > Exploring construction techniques > Prototyping

Footwear

Footwear has been created for centuries and many traditional construction techniques survive to this day. Lasts preserved from Roman times have provided clues into early shoemaking. Today, advanced technologies have made shoemaking faster but the principles of pattern making, cutting, fitting, lasting, bottoming and finishing (which we will explore further below) remain relatively unchanged. The needs of differently shaped and gendered feet continue to involve complex methods of construction.

Creating lasts

Creating a last from a single block of wood is possibly the most complex part of shoemaking, requiring years of practise in order to perfect the skill. Traditionally skilled craftspeople cut the last from wood. The last will be in the shape of the shoe's style, size and other characteristics. Completing this stage by hand is laborious and time consuming; however, modern machinery has somewhat shortened this process.

21–22. Using a range of plastic lasts, paper patterns begin to take the shape of shoes.

23. A first prototype gives the designer an opportunity to take a closer look at the proportion, size and fit of the shoes.

Computer-aided design has reduced the timescale even further. Lasts created by computer software can be altered and made in either wood or plastic. The adaptability of this method can provide designers with the flexibility to change styles very quickly. For both methods, for every shoe, size, foot, style and characteristic, a last must be made.

Pattern making

Pattern making for shoes involves making a two-dimensional pattern into a three-dimensional accessory. Flat patterns are needed to cut the leather pieces. A popular method used involves covering the last in masking tape and drawing the required design onto the covering. Cut along the style lines and carefully peel away the tape. Stick the pieces onto paper and recreate the patterns as flat pieces.

Grade the pattern pieces at this stage to create a range of standard sizes. For bespoke shoes, the last will create patterns that are unique to a specific person and which therefore cannot be graded for another person with different-sized feet. The patterns created at this stage are then used to make dies for mass production.

21

22

23

Cutting

Position the pattern pieces carefully onto the leather, avoiding imperfections in highly visible areas. Trace the patterns using chalk and label each piece to avoid confusion later. Cutting by hand, known as 'clicking', requires great care. Selecting appropriate areas on the leather is paramount, as each is different with weaker and stronger areas used for specific parts of the shoe. For cutting with dies, the pieces are cut out in several layers at once with automated machinery or by an operator.

Fitting

All the component parts for the upper are put together in the fitting room. Stitching can be completed by hand or machine and a plane used to thin layers from the seam allowance to reduce the thickness of the leather. The pieces are then sewn together, and any lining and interlining is added for warmth and comfort. Eyelets for shoelaces and small components too difficult to attach later are also completed.

Lasting

The fitted upper is stretched over the last and the shoe begins to take shape. Depending on the level of quality, closing the bottom of the shoe can be labour-intensive with many nails being needed to hold it in place. The upper is then stitched together or adhered with cement. Other component parts are also attached at this point.

Bottoming and finishing

Attaching the outsole to the shoe is called 'bottoming' and is a permanent process. The heel is then attached with glue and nails. Strength is the main requirement at this point because this part of the shoe receives the most wear and tear. To finish, the shoes are checked, cleaned and buffed. The leather is polished to create a shine and chemical solutions may be applied for extra protection and to waterproof the shoes.

Essential tools of the trade > Exploring construction techniques > Prototyping

Jewellery

Making jewellery is an ancient craft and the same principles and materials have been in use for thousands of years. Constructing jewellery is challenging, however, due to the nature of the materials used. Furthermore, working with metals and stones cannot be prototyped by pattern making as employed in other accessory construction. From simple wedding bands to very intricate necklaces with many joining parts, many of the construction techniques are unique to fine jewellery.

Turning metals into liquid form highlights the flexibility of this material. Precious stones, on the other hand, are not only expensive but also less pliable and so it is important to gain some prior training using cheaper stones for practise. We shall explore some basic techniques further below.

Cutting

There are several options available when cutting metal. Shears and guillotines are practical for large pieces; however, they are not suitable for intricate work because the pressure of the blades distorts the edges. The piercing saw is the tool of choice for many jewellers because of the accuracy it lends, although using it as a beginner may take some practise. The saw is so called because the blade is thin and can be threaded through a pilot hole onto the frame, thereby cutting holes from the inside. It is possible to position the saw to cut corners and curves, and tilting at an angle creates bevel edges. Remember: making long, full motions, the back stroke performs the actual cutting whilst the front stroke repositions the blade for the next cut.

Drilling

Drilling can make both small and large holes. Begin by marking a point to drill and then select a drill bit that is suitable for the metal or material. Place the work onto a steady, flat surface and hold it in place by hand if the work is very small, or place it on top of a piece of wood if using larger drill machinery. Always ensure that your piece of work is secure because the drill bit has the potential to move it as you work.

Filing

To smooth rough edges, to shape, or even out areas, filing removes metal slowly. Delicate work will require a fine file, whilst larger pieces can withstand a coarse file. Use hand files in slow, long strokes to ensure that large areas are not distorted at this stage. Once metal has been filed away, it is difficult to rectify mistakes.

Soldering

Solder melts at a low temperature and is used for joining metal. The liquid solder flows between the seams and is so light that it can defy gravity and flow upwards. Soldering must follow a process of cleaning, fluxing to keep the join clean, applying the solder, heating, cooling and finally cleaning the finished piece.

Hard soldering is preferable in jewellery making because of the strength and high proportion of precious metal in the solder. Apply flux to the joining area to keep it clean whilst working. The solder is placed onto the work and heat is applied, melting the solder and joining the pieces. With skill and attention, this method can provide an invisible, strong and permanent finish. After the piece has cooled, place it into a pickling solution and file away the excess solder.

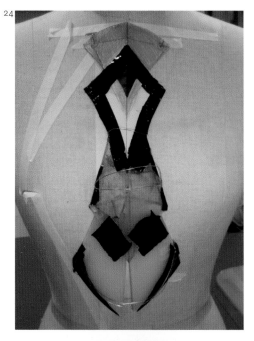

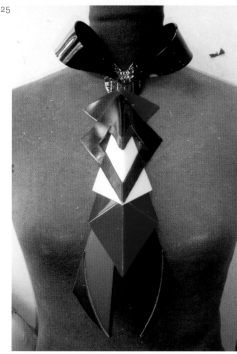

24–25. Kat Marks cuts perspex with precision and pieces it together to create dramatic examples of jewellery.

Bending

To avoid damaging the piece, the best method for bending is by hand; or use pliers if the metal or material is too strong. Metal is softened by the annealing technique: this involves heating the metal until it is pliable, which is usually indicated by a dull red colour. Allow the metal to cool slightly and bend. This method does not damage metal, but forcing stiff metals will make them become brittle and more likely to crack. Known as 'work hardening', metal hardens when worked with. Finally, of course, only ever bend hot metal with pliers.

Hammering

Different sized hammers are used for specific needs for a variety of materials. Wooden mallets flatten and stretch. Metal hammers have different uses for bending and smoothing surfaces. Practise by hammering metals and materials on different areas because metals react in distinctive ways. Hammering should always take place on a surface that can withstand the force. Remember: any marks on the hammer will transfer onto the metal; therefore, only use textured heads for a deliberate finish on the piece.

Finishing

The final step to completing jewellery is to treat the surface for the desired look. Rough metal is capable of a brilliant shine or a matt finish. Finishing will remove marks from hammering or from any of the processes, and should include smoothing edges for comfort and safety. Fine grades of sandpapers and files, as well as larger machines, can achieve a range of desired finishes.

26. These flexible gold bracelets by Krizia (Spring/Summer 2012) use carefully crafted joints that snap securely together to successfully accomplish a balance of function and decoration.

27. Mixing contemporary design and his trademark wit, Jean Paul Gaultier creates a solid choker featuring chains with functional clasps (Spring/Summer 2011).

Millinery

Creating simple or elaborate headwear requires sheer dexterity of the hand. Milliners also need to understand the two-dimensional and have a vision of the three-dimensional form – from flat patterns to the completed hat. Milliners have experimented with novel materials as they became available over the centuries, so that today hat making relies as much on the traditional raw materials of straw and felt as it does on metals, plastic and other synthetic materials, too. Creating a hat or cap requires moulding and building, with thousands of stitches and hundreds of hours of labour going into the most elaborate pieces.

28–32. In Stephen Jones's millinery studio, hat construction is in progress, using hat blocks to stretch and form fabric to create a three-dimensional headpiece.

28

30

29

31

32

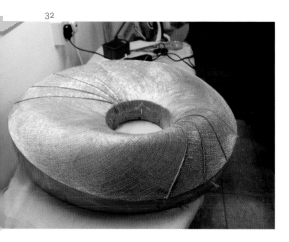

Creating patterns

Creating flat patterns can be difficult because of the nature of the accessory. Sectional crowns can be drafted if the exact head size is known. Start by dividing the head measurement into required sections, giving at least a three-centimetre (1.5-inch) ease allowance to ensure that the hat or cap is not too tight. Draw the height according to the measurement; begin curving the sections into arcs from seven centimetres from the length's edge. Cut out and place the flat pattern onto the block or head stand to check the shaping. To complete, make true the draft to create the final pattern, adding matching notches to the sides. Matching patterns, stripes or prints are completed at this stage.

To create the brim, draw around the correct-sized head plate. Depending on the size and shape required, draw the brim's edge marking both the centre front and centre back. Carefully cut out the middle section previously marked with the head plate and the outside edge. Place onto a head stand and begin by overlapping the centre back to create the curve of the brim. To curve the brim further, repeat the same technique at regular intervals and then make true the draft to create the pattern piece.

Blocking

Work out the grain of the fabric by locating the warp and weft threads and the bias, which gives a slight stretch on a 45° angle. Blocking is the act of hat making by placing fabric over the wooden block. Line the grain of fabric with the centre front and centre back. For many hats, there can be as many as three layers: the lining, foundation fabric to give structure, and the fashion fabric on the visible side.

Apply each layer of fabric separately by placing it over the block and then securing it with an elastic band. Soften the fabric with steam and secure the edge with pins. Leave the fabric to dry completely so that it stiffens and holds the shape of the crown. Repeat for each layer of fabric, then measure the depth of the crown accurately, mark along the edge with chalk and trim away the excess.

Stitching

Remove the crown from the block and backstitch along the trimmed edge to secure the three layers before covering the raw edge with bias tape. There are three methods for attaching the brim to the crown: the inside brim edge can lie over the crown, under the crown or be sewn right sides together and turned inside out. Select the most appropriate method and sew along with a strong hand-backstitch or machine stitch into place. Trim away the raw edges and hide the seam with a decorative feature. Insert a head ribbon inside for comfort, and sew bias tape or edge the brim with the same fabric to cover the raw edge.

Essential tools of the trade > **Exploring construction techniques** > Prototyping

Creating prototypes ensures that the specified shape and style of a piece is achieved using cheaper alternative materials that have the same properties (including the weight, thickness and strength) as those of the final material. For bags, card or felt is used instead of expensive leather. Using heavy paper and creating patterns on the last, prototypes for footwear can provide a visual guide of the final shoe. Making prototypes for jewellery is more difficult, but the piece should be well planned to avoid expensive mistakes. Hats can be made from card or inexpensive sinamay.

35

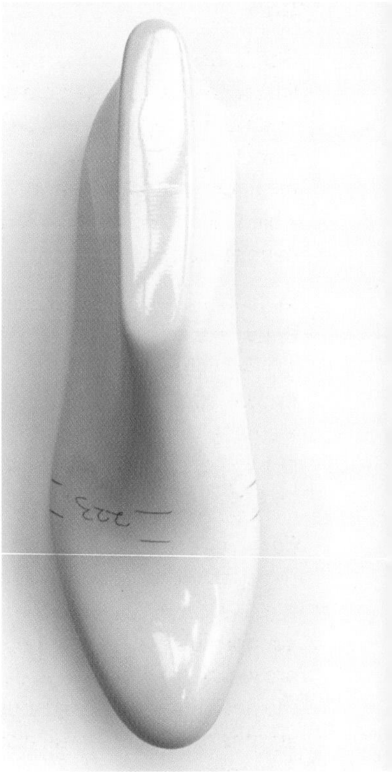

33

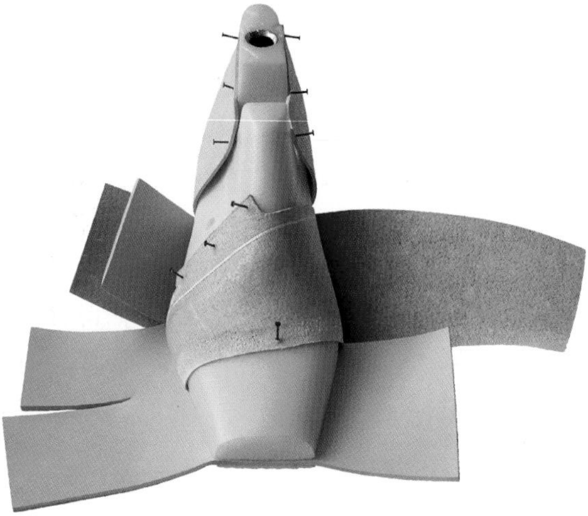

34

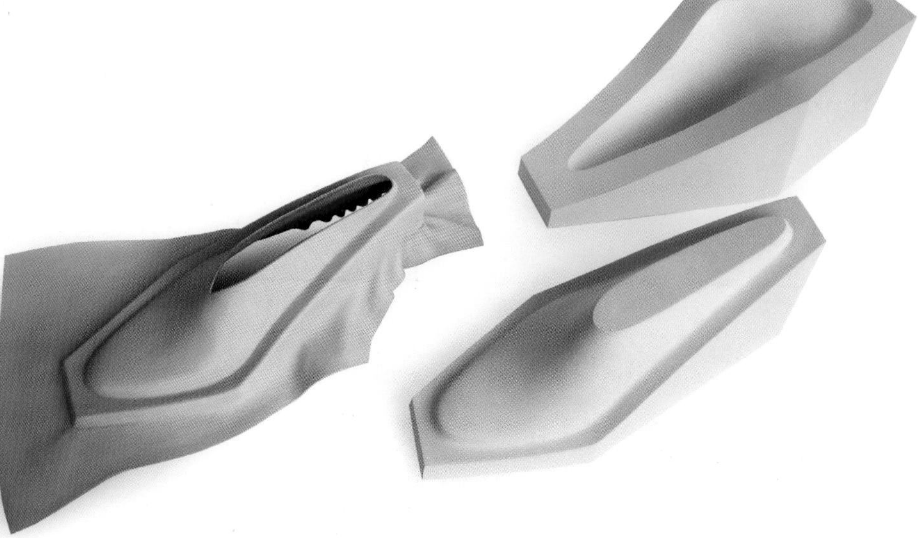

Size

Size is less important to bags and is usually limited to what the average person can carry or what the bag has been designed to do. Handbags may be designed to carry the minimum of objects, in contrast to holdalls, which must be able to carry a large number of possessions.

Making prototypes of shoes will help determine whether the size is correct before costly mistakes are made with cutting expensive leather. Grading is an important element to shoes for creating standard sizes or for bespoke footwear, when the sizes will be specific to the individual customer.

For jewellery, the key considerations are for rings, which have standardized sizes. Ensure that there is enough space for the wearer to comfortably manipulate the ring whilst they are wearing it. For necklaces, the fit around the neck is important; although the varying lengths of necklaces can also be for aesthetic reasons.

Hats must fit the head securely; therefore, measurements of the head should be taken carefully. A hat stretcher can adjust the size by careful steaming and stretching, although this must be used with caution to avoid misshaping. Caps can have adjustable straps to increase their flexibility and to reduce and extend their size.

Rapid prototyping

Rapid prototyping was first developed in the 1980s to speed up the process of constructing models and is now used by a wide variety of different industries. Virtual designs provide the basis of this technique by creating thin cross-sectional layers to create a virtual model. This method is used in engineering but is also applicable to many aspects of accessories production, especially commercial production. Rapid prototyping is a highly skilled area that can greatly reduce the time in which an accessory can be realized.

36

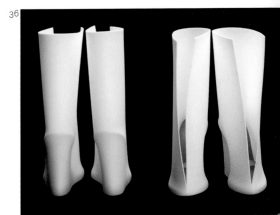

37

33–37. Marloes ten Bhömer uses rapid prototyping technology to create lasts and moulds for her innovative footwear designs.

Bespoke production

Bespoke production means one-of-a-kind pieces that are made entirely by hand, by machinery or by a combination of both methods. Bespoke production is important to the accessory industry because it is a means of making very personal items, some of which require thousands of hand stitches and hundreds of hours to make. Artisans throughout the world keep traditions alive by their practices in accessory making, with techniques that are centuries old.

Bags using fine leathers are cut individually and are often hand stitched throughout with their edges all finished to the highest standard. Hardware may be completely handmade and applied by hand to ensure a consistent quality of standards.

Footwear also uses fine leathers and is especially personal because of the individual sizes involved. Lasts are handcrafted to exact specifications and can accommodate both irregular-sized feet and personal tastes. Bespoke footwear incorporates hand stitching with hundreds of temporary and permanent nails used to hold the shoe's components in place.

The highly personal nature of jewellery can command the highest level of attention to detail. Engagement rings and wedding jewellery may employ the most expensive materials and stones for just one accessory. Occasionally, very large stones are cut into smaller pieces. Jewellery is regularly reconditioned or redesigned, with metals and stones recycled to create entirely new pieces.

38

Millinery, partnering with the couture industry, has a long history of bespoke production. Designers cater to individual customers, matching the design to personal tastes, occasions and head sizes. Expensive materials are commonly used in conjunction with finely detailed features.

process, but attaching features may have to be completed by hand because of intricate designs and hard-to-access areas. Some accessories are, however, made by one person from start to finish and jewellery is an example of this process due to the complexity of components that may require a higher level of skill to construct.

Commercial

The commercial mass market requires accessories to be produced quickly. On a production line, one operator may assemble one part of the bag, footwear, hat or cap. For bag production, machinists will sew pieces together whilst others are responsible for attaching hardware; constructing footwear is very similar. Millinery involves the same

38–39. A stark contrast is portrayed here between a commercial production facility, with its automated machinery, and a bespoke studio and its simple tools.

39

40

Beatrix Ong

In 2002, Beatrix Ong launched her shoe range which brings her signature aesthetic to the forefront of every design. She has quickly garnered the attention of celebrity fans with her critically acclaimed collections and has worked with the biggest names in the industry, including Martine Sitbon, Pringle and Temperley, and has now expanded her design talents with a range of luxury luggage for Globe-Trotter.

40–41. A whimsical and feminine high-heeled shoe from Beatrix Ong's recent collection.

What made you go into this dynamic industry?

I like the physical restrictions of the structure of a shoe and the challenge of having to design within these parameters. I didn't see it as an industry; just as something I really enjoy doing. The business developed as an offshoot of something I am passionate about.

Where does your inspiration originate?

People. I am very fortunate to meet so many different people and am always inspired by different cultures, beliefs and behaviours. My aim is to make people feel great – so it's only natural that they are my inspiration.

What is your design process?

I carry notebooks with me all the time – I sometimes carry up to three books. From lots of small sketches I develop them into drawings with the technical challenges in mind. From these I work out the shapes and group the collections within these kits. Finally, I develop the upper patterns on the last – this stage I am adamant on doing myself, as it not only saves time in development but it's also one of my favourite parts. When the prototypes are made, I then make any final alterations on a fit model to make sure it looks good on the foot.

41

Beatrix Ong

How and where do you source your materials and components?

The lasts and heels I develop in Italy where my manufacturing takes place. I source the materials from all over the world – it may sometimes be more complicated logistically, but it has always been worth it.

How do you work on your shapes?

The shapes are developed with both aesthetic and comfort in mind because it is important for me to achieve both in my products. I design the initial shapes on aesthetic and at the prototype stage we fit test them for comfort and then the samples go through another fit test before production. The shape may therefore have slight changes through its development, but they are minimal from conception.

How do you develop your range?

The range is determined by a combination of the logistics of production and what I feel tells the story of the brand best. Although you can have staples for each collection – boots in winter, open-toed shoes in summer – design-wise it comes down to what you want to communicate about your ideas. For example, I sometimes do a winter collection with a large number of evening shoes in the range, because I want to put across a feeling of celebration and cheer during the holiday season.

Where do you manufacture and why did you choose this place?

Italy. I chose the manufacturers I have because they are great people and make amazing products. I've worked with manufacturers from different parts of the world and no matter where they are, it is the connection with the people you work with that is important; when you are in factories for days on end, it makes the whole process an enjoyable one.

What should a new designer expect when embarking on their career in footwear?

Loving what you do is all important in any career. There are always challenges, peaks and troughs. Remembering why you do what you do gets you through the most difficult of times. Be prepared to keep on learning and remember, patience is always a virtue.

Construction techniques

42–44. Beatrix Ong's high-heeled shoes have balanced proportions and strong shapes which emphasize their playful details.

42

43

44

An example of humble millinery scaled to massive proportions, John Galliano adds humour and height with a giant pirate-style hat (Spring/Summer 2009).

Yarn is prepared by spinning and twisting fibres together, which makes it stronger than in its raw state. Climatic conditions affect the production of natural fibre and can seriously diminish the quality of the final product. Fibres are subjected to a long process to give the desired finish depending on the specific end-use.

Cellulose fibres

Cotton

USA, Russia and Pakistan are some of the largest cotton producers in the world. The finest-quality cotton, known as Sea Island cotton, is grown in the West Indies because of the favourable climate there. Cotton is characterized by the staple lengths: short lengths are coarser; the longer the staple, the smoother and more luxurious the handle.

Flax

The long fibre originates from the stem of the plant, called bast fibre. The length shortens when dried and is very absorbent of moisture. Fabric made from flax creases easily, although mixing it with other fibres and technological developments have produced better qualities in the handle and finish.

Protein fibres

Wool

Wool is one of the most versatile fabrics for weaving, knitting and felting. The fibre has a natural crimp and the properties are influenced by the type of wool, from the very coarse to soft and fine wool, such as merino. Fabric made from wool can have its creases removed naturally; or permanent creases can be created by applying specific finishing processes.

Silk

Wild silk fibres are irregular, creating fabric such as shantung silk, which has a distinctive uneven surface. Cultivated silk gives a very strong, lightweight, long and regular staple fibre when dry. The fibre is weakened when wet, requiring the user to handle the fabric with care.

1. Swathes of sea-blue silk envelopes a hat in waves by Jean Paul Gaultier for the Spring/Summer 2010 haute couture collection.

Woven fabrics

Plain woven fabrics have corresponding warp and weft threads that are the same vertically and horizontally. This type of weave is the most popular because of its strength and adaptability to a wide range of yarns. Lightweight fabrics using this method resist distortion by snagging. Decorative features may be incorporated into warp and weft threads, such as stripes.

There are two types of twill weaves, the 'S' and 'Z' twills. This type of weave creates its own distinctive pattern; the diagonal runs from either the left or right of the fabric. The pattern becomes more obvious in relation to how many of the weft threads float over the warp threads.

The main characteristic of the satin weave is the shine on the fabric created by long, floating threads. This method of weaving easily snags, distorting the fabric. The floating threads do not have the distinctive diagonal lines seen in twill weaves.

A pile, on pile fabrics, stands away from the weave and creates a nap, giving the fabric a soft-to-the-touch texture. The nap brushes in a particular direction, which affects how the pattern pieces should be cut. A pile that is pressed flat gives a luscious sheen to the fabric.

Knitted fabrics

Knitted fabrics are created with a series of interlinking loops from one yarn, making the fabrics highly flexible. Knitting machines can produce a wide range of knits, including warp and weft, and circular. Patterns can be created during the knitting process by adding colour and lace-like effects. Accessories using knitted fabrics may require special finishing processes, which may help support this easily distorted type of fabric.

Sourcing and sustainability

It is the responsibility of designers to incorporate sustainability in their accessories. To limit the negative impact that producing designs might have, sourcing materials responsibly is a long-term solution with positive benefits. There are five key benefits to sourcing sustainably: better design ensures that end-of-product life is specified; better working conditions for the workforce employed by accessories designers are guaranteed; harmful effects to the environment are minimized; implementing a cyclical design process to recycle waste reduces a designer's carbon footprint; and developing a profitable business enables further investment in future sustainability.

2. Jean Paul Gaultier cleverly uses a flutter of sheer silk to grandly rise above the model's head for his Autumn/Winter 2010–11 haute couture collection.

Natural fibres and fabrics > Natural skins

Humans have always used skin as a form of clothing and for accessories, partly out of necessity and partly as a means of adornment. The texture and thickness of natural skin depends on the animal. Cattle leather is tough yet versatile and can only stretch slightly. Many types of fur are very delicate. Using natural skin safely requires taking many things into consideration, the foremost being the welfare of the animal. It is important to remember that the use of skins has ethical implications and may not always be socially or culturally acceptable.

3

Leather

Leather has been hugely important to the footwear and bag industry. The most popular leather is cattle hide that has been tanned and, usually, the younger the animal, the less damage that takes place to the skin during this process. There are two sides to leather, which are indicated by the texture of the surface. The appearance of leather can easily be altered by many different methods, such as hot plating to smooth the surface, and embossing to imitate other types of skins.

Fur

Fur used in fashion includes that of the beaver, chinchilla, ermine, fox, mink, muskrat, nutria (also known as 'swamp rat' in the US), otter, rabbit and sable. It is only in recent times that the hair of the fur has been worn on the outer side; previously, fur was worn on the inside for warmth. Fur is graded according to quality and should be checked for patches, which are indicative of stress. Fur has two layers, with the coarse top layer called the 'guard hairs' and the denser, softer layer called 'undercoat hairs'. Sew pieces of fur together with a whipstitch, then gently pull open, flattening the edges to meet.

Main stages of leather preparation

Flaying and preserving
Untreated skin, known as greenhide, is checked for quality and defects. Salted or dried skin is called rawhide.

Beamhouse
In this area, the skin is soaked and rehydrated in special solutions to take away unwanted layers and hair; it also undergoes a process of fleshing to remove unwanted flesh and fat.

Tanning
This process turns the skin into leather by adding tanning agents, which produce specific desired qualities, before it is then sorted again according to quality and defects.

Dressing
This stage transforms tanned leather into finished leather. For equal thickness, the leather is divided into two: the upper side is called the 'grain' and the flesh side is called the 'split'. The final processes for this stage include stretching (formally called 'the setting-out process'), staking to soften the leather and buffing to create different types of leather, such as suede.

Finishing
The leather is finished by either spraying or padding to complete the process.

4

3. After centuries of popularity, fur continues to adorn people's accessories and to create spectacular statements such as that pictured here, which featured as part of Shiatzy Chen's Autumn/Winter 2012–13 collection.

4. Leather is a very popular choice for many accessories designers, including Marc Jacobs for his Autumn/Winter 2012–13 collection, because of its versatile properties, durable quality and flexibility for many uses.

Bill Amberg

Bill Amberg continues the long British tradition of designing and producing the finest leather bags and accessories. He is renowned and recognized internationally for his exquisite work with leather. His designs push new boundaries, incorporating inspirational techniques with new types of materials. Bill is a dynamic designer backed by a strong heritage, which is clearly evident in every accessory piece he designs.

6

7

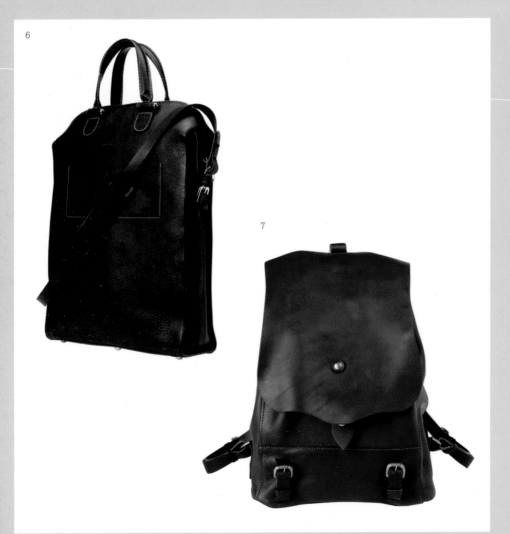

Materials

Why did you choose to design accessories?

This all began with studying in Australia. I worked with craftsmen as an apprentice and ensured that this covered every part of leather craft, including saddlery. When I returned to the United Kingdom with my experience, it was natural to move into accessories design. I fully appreciate that leather work is very different from using other materials and that you need a full background to know what it can do for you.

Where do your ideas originate?

From a very broad base and from curiosity. I pick around from films, photography and going to art galleries. All ideas in life can be inspiring. There is also the practical side to think about – considering what people need and how accessories can fit into their lives. For example, compared to almost a decade ago bags have become progressively smaller again because new technologies such as tablet computers and mobile phones have reduced in size. All these needs are incorporated into each bag because this is what the customer requires.

What is your design process?

The design process will always begin by sketching with a pencil on paper. To be able to draw is vital to design because this formalizes the ideas onto the page. The ideas are taken to the benches where craftspeople will work on the prototypes, or I use my studio at home to make them. This is an ongoing process that is continually evolving. For me, the actual making is also part of the design process. There is also a very technical side to design that must be incorporated into the process.

What inspires your colour palette each season?

I go to Première Vision, as well as all the trade fairs and leather shows to check out the new colours that are on offer. I look at what is coming up as a trend by seeing what the fashion-led tanneries are offering and producing. Colour can add a layer to the leather and then there is also the finishing, from smooth to glazed to waxed, which gives us new ideas.

How do you develop your range?

The range is developed according to a merchandising plan, although there will be apex pieces and drop-ins to complement the range. The range is carefully planned from the formal to the fashionable and tends to fit into the price triangle. We are known for producing long-lasting pieces, and although not quite trend-led, the range is always open to new trends. We have to think about the customer and their needs.

What types of materials do you use?

I use a lot of vegetable-tanned leathers, which give a depth to the look of the leather. I avoid using heavily pigmented leathers or printed grains because they do not look natural. I also use many other types of materials, including canvases, wool and felt. I am currently working with nylon with waterproof leather and this is a very exciting development at the company.

5. Bill Amberg

6–7. Two working bags showcase the skill of a master craftsman with a talent for design, demonstrating Bill Amberg's understanding of fine leather.

8–9 (overleaf). Bill Amberg manipulates the finest grade leathers to create two traditional-looking holdalls.

Bill Amberg

Do you experiment with new types of materials?

Experimenting with new types of materials is important. So much is driven by modern technology. Working on the waterproof line, incorporating the leathers and nylon, has given us the chance to develop our manufacturing techniques. We have used No-Sew Technology, such as welded and seam tapes, to completely seal the seams. I am inspired by all different areas that are completely unrelated to fashion and accessories. There is so much to learn from shoe technology and even from the technology for tents. Some of the most inspiring developments have come from hot-air balloons – the idea of the seaming and construction of these structures is very inspirational.

What can a new designer learn from your experience with experimenting with materials?

The variety of the leathers out there is vast and at first glance could be viewed as very simple, but so much still needs to be understood. There is so much to learn about the raw materials and the variety on offer. A new designer needs to experiment with a leather, firstly by making products using it, in order to fully understand how it works.

Leather is a by-product of the food industry and is truly sustainable and biodegradable. With reliable tanneries, you can trace the provenance of every skin. We have come so far, but are as yet unable to find a suitable alternative to leather. Nothing matches those natural characteristics and using fake leather is damaging because of the materials and processes involved to make them, which are damaging to the environment.

8

Where do you manufacture your accessories?

Some work is completed right here in the studio. We have factories in the United Kingdom that produce for us because English leather goods have long been at the forefront of style and there is a solid foundation of understanding, knowledge and skill of how it is created – we know what works well. This has come from our very long history of equine tradition and shoe making that has informed us of the making of leather goods. It is exactly this style that is very difficult to replicate and compared to others around the world, it is very obvious that English leatherwork is the best for our purposes because of the high level of craftsmanship. We also use Spain to manufacture because their methods are the closest to what we find in the United Kingdom and they also have a long tradition of making leather goods.

What do you find inspiring when working on collaborative projects?

I find it very inspiring to be working with other people on collaborative projects and having ideas for other people too. There are limitations to working on these projects as each person will have their own ideas; therefore, designing for other people will always have its parameters. I have worked with other parts of the industry because leather is used so widely that it touches almost everyone's life, from their shoes to their car interiors. We also do so much more. The Bill Amberg Studio has very active product development and interiors departments, working with many companies to produce bespoke pieces. We have also worked with the car, cycling, hotel and restaurant industries, to name a few. Each will bring a fresh idea and I try to tap into their thinking to produce what is needed.

9

Metals

The most common metals used in high-quality accessories are gold, silver and platinum. These materials are utilized extensively in jewellery, and other accessories have taken advantage of their malleability for components and features. These natural materials require careful consideration, especially when creating jewellery, as the wearer must be comfortable with the metal used, which must not react with the skin after prolonged contact. When designing accessories that incorporate metals as components, always ensure that they are very hard wearing.

Fine gold is very soft and classified as 24 carat (ct) (US karat/kt), with 18ct meaning 18 parts gold to six parts another metal; this classification further reduces to 9ct (i.e. nine parts gold to 15 parts another metal, forming an alloy), which is much harder. Fine silver has excellent malleable properties and is very reflective, although it tarnishes easily when the metal comes into contact with sulphur in the air. Sterling silver has 925 parts to 1,000 parts of fine silver.

Platinum is an extremely strong metal; it resists corrosion and tarnishing very well, and does not wear away easily compared with gold. Other metals, such as copper and brass, work well in many types of accessories; however, they do not retain the polish well and tarnish easily. Alloys are a mixture of metals that are created especially for strength and hardness.

Stones

Precious stones, because of their rarity, epitomize fine jewellery. They are sorted according to their quality. Other accessories have also incorporated the use of precious stones, such as in buckles for bags and shoes. Stones require great skill to cut and it takes apprentices years to master the techniques required in order to show off their brilliance.

Not all stones are of the finest quality – many have small inclusions (flaws) that affect their final quality. The more inclusions a stone has, the less it will shine, resulting in a dull-looking stone. Stones with few inclusions are considered rare and are therefore expensive. The best examples in circulation today are cut into round, square, baguette and pear shapes and designers need to consider the correct settings to securely hold a stone in place.

Commonly used stones in jewellery

Diamonds, emeralds, rubies and sapphires are considered precious stones.

Diamonds are the hardest stones in the world and their use is regarded as the pinnacle of fine jewellery.

Emeralds are usually green in colour and have many inclusions due to their poor resistance to breakage.

Rubies are known for their distinctive colour, red, which comes in many shades.

Sapphires are related to rubies and have many other qualities; they are also used in other industries due to their hardness.

Amber, garnet, lapis lazuli, opal and pearl are considered semi-precious stones.

10. John Galliano for Dior brings together the theatrical and historical with glistening colossal stones for the Spring/Summer 2010 haute couture collection.

The materials that are commonly used in accessories today have taken inspiration from other industries and have subsequently been developed in ways that are designed to bring increased comfort and style to the user. New areas of development in the twenty-first century particularly focus on the search for faster methods to make smarter materials using biotechnology or cleaner plastics.

Smart fabrics

Smart fabrics are created using a mixture of traditional fabric construction methods with new technological approaches. An LED (or light-emitting diode) produces a powerful source of light with low heat emissions. If embedded into fabric, the light can change according to the programmed information, allowing the designer to alter the colours and patterns it generates and so suit seasonal needs and trends.

Fibre-optic lights are also good for accessories designers to experiment with. Specialist lighting companies manufacture both woven and knitted fabrics which incorporate them. Additionally, fibre-optic cables can be cut and inserted into the fabric in order to produce a pile fabric. These types of smart fabrics are used primarily on the outside for decorative purposes, but can also be developed for functional purposes, such as for the lining of a bag to illuminate its interior.

Biotechnology

The natural environment is also inspiring new advances in biotechnology and the search to harness potential new sources of fibres. Spider silk, for instance, is incredibly strong and elastic in comparison to steel but proves expensive to produce because the fibre requires time and many spiders to yield enough silk to produce a length of cloth.

Plastic

Plastic is melted at a high temperature and is shaped using either injection moulding or sheets that are heated until pliable over a form. Plastic has properties that are suitable for making lightweight sculpted shapes for all types of accessories. Furthermore, this flexible material is becoming ever safer and more environmentally friendly through the development of recycled and upcycled previously used plastic. Although plastic is not a new material, processes are advancing all the time and designers are constantly discovering the incredible practicality of the material with each new development.

11

12

13

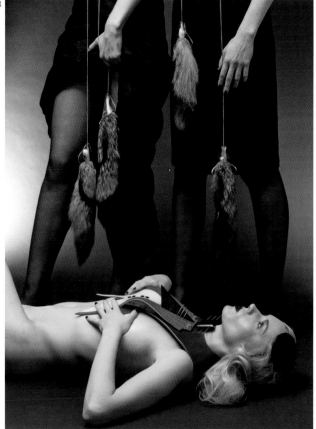

11–13. An innovative use of plastic is displayed in these sculpted plastic neckpieces by contemporary designer, Kat Marks, whose work explores the possibilities of manipulating a malleable material.

Natural metals and stones > **New developments** > Industry perspective

15

14. Alena Akhmadullina uses layered strips of plastic with embedded jewel colours to create a holographic effect for this stunning necklace (Spring/ Summer 2012).

15. For his Spring/Summer 2008 haute couture Dior collection, John Galliano's millinery was designed to look space-age-like with this futuristic helmet made in moulded plastic. The three-dimensional intricate designs covered in gilt sit flush within the main lines of the helmet.

Marloes ten Bhömer

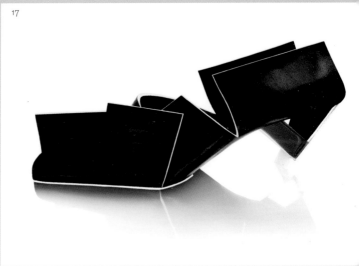

The internationally renowned and critically acclaimed designer produces footwear that is described as provocative and other-worldly. Marloes ten Bhömer has firmly established her signature of infusing technological advances into creative experiments to produce innovative shoes.

What made you decide to join this industry?

While studying product design at the ArtEZ, in the Netherlands, I was introduced to footwear design by one of my tutors, Marijke Bruggink, founder of the shoe label Lola Pagola.

Within my role as product designer, I find shoes a very interesting and complex subject matter. Shoe design involves the full spectrum of design concerns, from material knowledge to engineering and highly intuitive aspects. My own design concerns focus on designing objects that ignore or criticize conventions in order to make the product world less generic. Shoes also need to be structurally sound. Making shoes in a non-conventional way and still making them technically accurate a real challenge.

In addition to these challenges, I am very drawn to the fact that shoes, by being very close to the body, have a strong influence on the person wearing them, both physically and emotionally.

What inspires you to create your contemporary designs?

My work consistently aims to challenge generic typologies of women's shoes through experiments with non-traditional technologies and material techniques. By reinventing the process by which footwear is made, the resulting shoes serve as unique examples of new aesthetic and structural possibilities, while also serving to criticize the conventional status of women's shoes as cultural objects.

Materials

18

19

What is your design process?

There are a few ways in which I start the process of creating a piece: changing and adopting a process/material (from outside the footwear industry) for the production of shoes; translating a sketch/mock-up into a suitable material and process that would structurally work; draping/folding/pressing material around an existing last or foot to create a design; then translating this into a suitable material (sometimes the same material used for the mock-up model).

More recently, my starting points are more conceptual and deal with ideas that I am working through about manufacturing, structure and methodology, which I may go on to translate into an object or installation.

In the case of 'Rotational moulded shoe' (image 21, overleaf), the technical innovation and the use of a mechanical making process play a role in the concept of the After Hours installation. This work serves as a critique on the aesthetic and extrinsic value of mechanically produced objects versus handmade objects.

How do you develop your range?

I never work with ranges. My main aim with my work is to get away from conventional style clichés and codes, such as sporty, girly, feminine and so on. Rather than designing shoes based on customer profiling, which I think mostly leads to stereotyped footwear, my approach to footwear is to use materials and technologies to discover the shoe anew. Designing ranges would take time away from innovating and doesn't really apply to my way of working. Ideas that I have for constructions and detailing do evolve over time and sometimes inform the next design, but I wouldn't call them ranges.

16. Marloes ten Bhömer.

17–19. The unique qualities of Marloes ten Bhömer's footwear designs lie in the unusual use of folded leather and moulded plastic.

New developments > Industry perspective

Marloes ten Bhömer

Why is the prototype stage important to you?

My research into feet and footwear has resulted in a variety of experimental conceptual pieces, some of which have been developed into technically sound (wearable) shoes, whilst others are produced solely as sculptural pieces. The existence of both directions within my practice generates layers to my work that comment on the perception of functionality. The context within which they sit (in galleries, museums, or in boutiques) challenges the audience's preconceptions about the shoe.

What types of materials inspire you and why?

It isn't so much materials themselves that inspire me, but what they mean in cultural terms – where they come from, how they can be processed and what they can achieve aesthetically and structurally. I am mostly interested in materials/processes that have an interesting relation to efficiency and might even be counter-intuitive, such as rotational moulding and rapid prototyping.

What can a new designer learn from your experience with experimenting with materials?

I think that experimentation with materials can hugely inform an object both aesthetically and in terms of function. Experimentation and innovation is something that can be done with materials that are common and specialist, processed both in-house and in collaboration with industry.

One example of a technique that I invented is a leather-laminating, leather-mâché technique. It is a translation of a technique that most of us learn in school – papier-mâché – making it an example of DIY experimentation.

With leather-mâché, no pattern developing time is required and the wall thickness can be varied. This allows for a shoe to be made that exactly traces the form of the foot on the inside, allowing the external silhouette to differ from the convention of the foot.

20

21

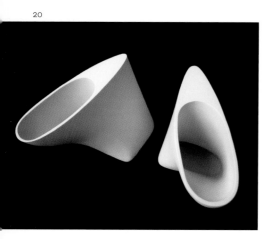

Where do you source your materials from?

I use a wide variety of materials ranging from carbon fibre, polyurethane resin, stainless steel and leather to glass fibre. They are used in different industries, but are mostly widely accessible.

What can you learn from working on collaborative projects?

First and foremost you learn whether you are fit to collaborate! I think the most interesting thing about collaborating is learning to understand questions and challenges from a wide variety of fields, both in terms of how they might overlap with your own specialism and also how they can inform it.

What advice can you give a new designer establishing their career in accessory design?

I think that it is very important to understand the context in which you operate and want to operate in and the role you have or might aspire to. It is important to know what you want to be doing on a day-to-day basis. Not all contexts have a platform yet. You might need to create it yourself.

Although I design shoes, I wouldn't necessarily say that my field of work is the fashion industry. The context of my work varies from fashion, design, crafts, art and sometimes technology.

20–23. These footwear designs by Marloes ten Bhömer utilize advanced technology and forward critical thinking to challenge conventional shoe design through the use of these moulded pieces.

22   23

n Paul
design,
f subtle
t
rt of
haute

Hand finishing is labour-intensive and costly, but produces results that are difficult to replicate. One person, or a team of people, might spend hundreds of hours completing just one accessory. Techniques traditionally used to embellish quality pieces continue to be employed today because of the ongoing demand for special and unique accessories. Intricate and detailed surface finishes, in both flat and three-dimensional forms, are frequently found in high-end accessories, as we shall explore further below.

Textile surface finishes

Beads and sequins of all sizes produce a luxurious effect. Different sized beads create texture, whilst layering sequins reflects light depending on the density of the embellishment. To reduce the intensive labour required for sewing each embellishment individually, pre-strung beads and sequins are affixed onto the fabric using a tambour hook to pull up a loop of thread, before then anchoring each thread to form a chain stitch on the reverse side.

Appliqué is a technique that simply involves sewing layers of fabric together or layering textures. Graduating from the very subtle to the bold in contrasting backgrounds, begin with transferring the design onto the right side of the fabric. Pieces of fabric that fray will require seam allowances and must be worked under the design for a smooth finish. Seam allowances for fabrics that do not fray are not necessary.

Passementerie is a highly embellished form of embroidery that uses trims such as cord, ribbon and braid to produce distinctive patterns, thereby creating unusual surfaces. Carefully apply the trims with a couching stitch to secure the pieces, ensuring that corners are flat and curves are smooth.

Finishes

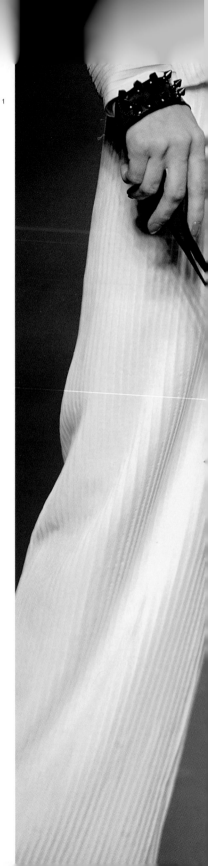

Metal surface finishes

Engraving involves cutting metal away from a surface in order to create patterns and inscriptions. Depending on how deep the craftsperson makes the cut, various different effects can be produced. You will need to polish the surface prior to transferring the design onto the accessory. Create grooves by placing the cutting tool (called the graver) directly onto the line and cut. Work on small sections, brushing away the excess curls of metal.

Stamping is an old technique used for adding texture to metal. Impressions are created in the metal by using punches and hammers with predetermined patterns. This technique is similar to embossing, although the design does not appear on the reverse side of the accessory. Interesting effects can be created using this method, although making prototypes may help you to gauge the exact amount of pressure required to create the desired look.

1. A handbag with decorative studs by Jean Paul Gaultier for his Spring/Summer 2011 haute couture collection.

Hand embellishments > **Machine embellishments**

With the advent of the industrial revolution, machinery was invented to mimic many jobs traditionally completed by hand. These new machines sped up production and for the first time in history created accessories that looked exactly the same as each other, were of consistent quality and made to a high standard. Technology has further advanced since then, and digital technology can now design and manufacture highly embellished designs for a fraction of the price and time as previously.

2. Machine-embroidered creative handbag by contemporary bag designer, Lee Mattocks, which creates an image with tonal threads and completes the bag with rabbit fur trim.

3. The spindly lace-like detailing on this bag by Jean Paul Gaultier for his Spring/Summer 2012 haute couture collection sharply contrasts with the acidic colour of the leather.

2

Embroidery

Free machine embroidery creates either abstract or clearly defined patterns to make an image, motif or logo. Industrial embroidery machines, also known as Irish machines, produce excellent quality surface embellishments very quickly. Digital embroidery machines digitize an image and select colours by reducing the amount of them required. The sewing is automated and uses a diverse range of threads, from those that are very thick and create a textured surface, to metal threads, such as those used in Chinese embroidery.

Incorporating embroidery in accessory design is commonplace. Silk thread has been popular in embroidery throughout history and lends a rich quality to the final piece of work. A designer should always endeavour to experiment with different fabrics and materials, such as dissolvable fabric for instance, which is embroidered and then dissolved in water, leaving just the interlinking threads to create a web-like effect.

Printing

Printing techniques have greatly advanced to produce significantly better quality designs. Digital patterns created using computer-aided design provide the designer with the flexibility to use much more colour than with traditional screen-printing done by hand and achieved with inks. Printing gives further opportunities to develop designs not limited by traditional methods. Digital printing enables patterns to be printed directly onto the fabric in the exact shape of the accessory, for instance, thereby minimizing wastage.

Contemporary finishing techniques continually develop with advances in technology and designers constantly experiment with hand and machine techniques to complete accessories. The techniques they use will be incorporated into the accessory's design and will therefore be applied to the fabric, leather or materials prior to the construction of the final accessory.

4. Layered laser cutting adds a delicate effect to the trims on these boots by designer Jody Parchment.

4

Cutting

Laser cutting cuts out components using a mixture of gases to generate a highly heated laser beam. Initially developed for industrial needs, the accessories industry has experimented with this method of finishing to produce accurately cut patterns on even the strongest of materials, including metal. The design is created using vector-based creative software, which guides the laser beam on a predetermined track. The intense heat from the beam also seals edges. This type of cutting produces consistent quality and standards.

Heat and gas free, water-jet cutting is better for some types of work and materials. This method cuts using a highly accurate and pressurized focused stream of water, which can also be mixed with an abrasive. The jet of water passes through a nozzle made of precious stone to cut through a range of materials, from marble and stone to soft rubber. This type of technique cuts through thicker materials, or more layers of them, than does laser cutting.

5

5. Intricate laser cutting provides a glimpse of the wearer through the stencil-like boot, which rests on a heavy, gilded base.

6

6. The pastel blue snakeskin provides a soft background for the engraved gold plate mounted on the front of these shoes, which featured as part of Yves Saint Laurent's Spring/Summer 2012 collection.

7. Traditional embroidery is fused with modern precision laser cutting for these high-heeled boots in John Richmond's Autumn/Winter 2012–13 collection.

Michelle Lowe-Holder

Michelle Lowe-Holder began her career in the fashion industry after graduating from the prestigious Pratt Institute in New York. After a mentoring programme for sustainable fashion in London, her design direction shifted. Michelle's fine vintage and heritage handcraft detail incorporate her efforts to be sustainable and her determination to practice zero waste, by upcycling using end of lines and scraps from previous collections, known as 'cabbage'.

8–10. Michelle Lowe-Holder practises sustainable design by using finds from various sources. Her pieces are carefully handcrafted with precision folds that are designed to flex and so become an integral part of the wearer.

9

Why did you decide to join this dynamic industry?

I started collecting vintage clothes at 12 and knew from this age I would be involved in fashion or costumes. I still have these pieces and they are still just as beautiful to me as they were then. I love the craftsmanship and making involved. It is a passion that kind of chooses you – it was never a difficult decision.

What inspires you to create your contemporary designs?

I am inspired by anything; it could be a Victorian vintage pin-cushion detail; a photo from 1850s America; a museum exhibition or just a person that you see in a park; there is no set rule because I am always looking.

What is your design process?

From the inspiration it is translated into a fabric design detail such as print, manipulation or painting. This design is then explored and developed – until it can form into the accessory I am looking for. The process is very organic and fuels itself, following a process of make, look, change, make, look and change. There is always an element of surprise, as materials themselves will influence the direction and often the aesthetic of the final design.

10

Michelle Lowe-Holder

Why is the prototype stage important?

You cannot design without prototypes – even if you start from sketches. The techniques used, materials and finish all have to be realized in prototype form to work out problems and direction.

What types of materials inspire you?

I consider myself an 'eco-hybrid' brand. I upcycle/recycle using zero waste techniques and off-cuts. I also use end-of-line vintage textiles and ribbons. However, I cannot always use sustainable materials as they are not always available – for example, I have not been able to find 'eco-hardware'.

What can a new designer learn from experimenting with materials?

There are many ways to design – from research, draping, sketching and conceptualizing. Experimenting with materials is another way of actualizing ideas in a very organic way, which as a new designer you will always need to do.

Where do you source your materials?

I am a true magpie, collecting to an obsessive level. I buy from markets, end-of-line wholesalers, warehouses and vintage shops. I also buy from a sustainable fabric company in Italy. I reuse a lot of off-cuts from my own collections, from my personal stock and also from a factory in East London.

What do you learn from collaboration?

I love collaborative projects because it is interesting to have new input from another source. I always gain from collaboration as you can always learn from it; being in the studio and constantly being so focused can narrow your vision – but collaboration keeps you open. It is very interesting to have your working boundaries and goals set from another point of view.

What advice would you give a new designer?

Get ready for a bumpy ride!

11

11–15. The challenges of practising eco- and ethical design are not obvious at first glance, but each accessory has a history as well as a story to tell. These examples of handcrafted jewellery by Michelle Lowe-Holder showcase her style, which includes both chunky and delicate pieces.

Finishes

12

14

13

15

Developing finishing techniques that work for accessories design requires both practise and experimentation. Many finishing techniques are capable of crossing boundaries and being incorporated into other accessories. Using a mixture of hand- and machine-finishing techniques allows layering and combinations for richer designs. Using materials that are uncommon to a given type of accessory can produce interesting and surprising effects.

16–18. Sketchbooks are invaluable resources from which to collect inspiration, ideas and notes. They can serve to remind the designer of the key themes in a collection during the development stages of the design process. Shown here are sketchbook pages inspired by the artist Otto Dix.

16

17

18

Objective and learning outcome

Art has inspired accessories designers for decades, from colours to patterns and images. The purpose of this activity is to make you think about seeking inspiration from art movements or artists and to encourage you to look at individual artworks that you find intriguing or inspiring in order to further develop your own research and ideas.

Design task

Begin by using an artist's work for inspiration and recreate the artwork that you have chosen in an abstract form by scaling up specific areas. Stencil images onto fabric that does not fray, or onto leather if you prefer, and then cut out small sections of the image. Emboss the remaining uncut areas to create more texture. Apply these new techniques to different accessories that you are working on to create a coherent theme throughout.

Employing a creative blend of fabrics can also serve to produce dynamic imagery. The randomness of this technique can produce unique design features that are equally suitable for use with bags, footwear or millinery. Recreating the image requires studying both lighter and darker shades, then selecting fabric according to colour and pattern. Darker shades will need stronger colours and denser patterns, whilst lighter shades will require the opposite.

It is also worth experimenting with colour printing on soft textiles; or try enamelling metal, which produces a range of exciting combinations and effects.

19

Since his debut in 2007, Justin Smith Esq. has set out to create both classic hats and creative couture pieces. His millinery has been a critical success and has been recognized with both an i-D Styling Award and the Maria Luisa award at IT86. Justin's extraordinary vision matches his passion for upholding traditional skills, which is evidenced in his designs for Moschino, Manish Arora and Carolyn Massey.

What inspires you most in millinery?

I take my inspiration from anything that I see. Nature inspires me a great deal. My work is very technique-based, so my collections reflect a seed idea that has been developed through pushing the boundaries of techniques within millinery.

Where does your inspiration originate?

A starting point for a seed idea can start from anywhere. My Shade collection was based on a book, *Neverwhere* by Neil Gaiman; and my Air collection was based on an idea inside my head that went: 'Wouldn't that look great with a parrot on the top!' (see image 25, overleaf).

What is your design process?

I develop techniques through an understanding of the craft of millinery and then push them to the limit, developing new ideas about the way that things are made and worn.

19–25. Justin Smith Esq. modernizes historical influences for his millinery, to create both perfectly pitched simple pieces and highly extravagant hats.

20

21

How do you develop your shapes?

I look a lot at vintage hats, vintage silhouettes... I love the Edwardian era, so a lot of my silhouettes start there, along with the techniques.

How do you develop your range?

I try and offer a range that is neither masculine nor feminine. It's an exploration of being able to offer a luxury bespoke product that will be worn with style and get better with age and love. I try to offer a range that covers everything from occasional showpieces to everyday hats.

What can you learn from working on collaborative projects?

I collaborate a lot and it's great to work with other designers who have dreams of what they want to say. Being an accessories designer, you have to understand the designer you're working with – get in their head, create what they want, but do it in a way that looks great and represents the best quality that you can achieve. It's a completely different way of working than simply fulfilling my own fantasies within my collections.

What do you find most inspiring when making bespoke pieces?

I love making one-off pieces – such as a really special hat – for something and somebody special; you know that no one will have the same hat, ever. I love working with people; this comes from having previously worked as a[n award-winning] hairdresser. So whether it is a one-off hat for a client, or a bigger job for a designer, they are all special hats made with love for special people.

Do you think that millinery will continue to be an important part of a person's wardrobe?

Hats are a great way to give yourself style and show discernment. A great hat can last for years; it can also be mended and adjusted as needed over the years, just like in the old days! People often think that hats are only for special occasions; but style is a daily thing.

22

23

Justin Smith Esq.

24

25

Cacharel mix and matches bright tones for the Spring/ Summer 2011 collection for their vintage-style sunglasses with radiant lenses and translucent frames.

Long regarded throughout history as a sign both
of authority and intellectual superiority, glasses
(also known as 'spectacles') were originally
created as a means of correcting eyesight and
offering wearers a clearer picture of the world
around them. Glasses are created by inserting
corrective lenses in a variety of thicknesses,
curvatures and angles into frames. Today, vanity
eyewear has exploded in popularity amongst
those not requiring glasses for medical reasons,
making the accessory no longer one of mere
necessity, but one that is also highly fashionable
and desirable.

1

Glasses

Although once fashionable and extensively used, expensive horn and tortoiseshell (which are lightweight and have a highly polished finish) have completely fallen out of use due to both ethical and legal reasons surrounding the sale of these materials. Frames are now largely made from materials such as metal and plastic, which are popular because the materials are easy to work with when hot, are malleable and are also extremely robust and so able to withstand constant wear.

The design of eyewear is limited to what the ears and nose can comfortably hold. Begin the design process by mapping these limitations, along with other important considerations, such as the intended thickness of the lens and shape of the face. Frames which are to be used for medical reasons must be hard wearing and the lens will be required to fit securely into the frame, therefore consider the thickness and shape of the lens in relation to the frame. Generally, a lens with a large surface area will have thicker edges; however, advanced technology has made lenses much thinner.

Consider how the glasses will fold together, which is usually enabled by hinges on the arms. A frame made from metal or plastic relies on small screws to hold it together and perhaps also springs for added flexibility. Frameless glasses, on the other hand, are held together by the bridge, arms and thin wire that fits inside the groove of the lens.

1. These futuristic bug-eye inspired glasses and sunglasses circa 1960s radically alter the proportion and shape of the face.

2. Oversized, frameless and moulded from a single lens, these Fendi sunglasses (Spring/Summer 2012) do not obstruct the outline of the shape of the face yet still make a bold statement.

Sunglasses

Tinted lenses have come to represent a commanding sub-sector of the main eyewear market. Sunglasses provide protection for the eyes, filtering both daylight and ultra-violet light. Fashion trends dictate changing styles of frames and lenses, which can range from dark to light graduations to multiple colours. Consider the implications of using tinted lenses because of the dangers involved: pilots shielding their eyes from sun glare will have different requirements from the average user, for instance.

2

Eyewear > Scarves

The scarf can be traced back to very humble origins. Romans routinely used the sudarium, which literally translates to 'sweat cloth', which was made from linen and was designed to keep them clean by soaking up sweat in hot weather. The scarf has remained a practical item today but is principally used as a way of keeping warm in cold climates. The scarf can have many functional uses, including as a means of keeping dust and fumes out of the mouth and nose in dry, arid deserts, for instance. There are several common types of scarf in use that are worn on different parts of the body.

Past and present uses

Scarves have been worn for many reasons, most notably for religious purposes as a means to express the rank and importance of the person wearing the accessory. Scarves are not just worn around the neck; a headscarf, for instance, is symbolic in many religions, including Islam. The mantilla, made from lace, continues to be worn by Catholics in Spain. The military have also used scarves made from linen, cotton and silk to signify the status or position of a given individual. The academic scarf identifies the university of the wearer through its pattern, design or insignia, and is especially popular with historically eminent institutions, such as the University of Cambridge or Harvard University.

3

3. A medical-style neck brace inspires this scarf featuring thick padding by Balenciaga for its Autumn/Winter 2007 collection.

4. The extreme limits of the knitted scarf were explored through the use of heavy, thick yarn by Giles as part of his striking Autumn/Winter 2007 collection.

4

Design

The scarf is arguably the most simple of all accessories to manufacture. The shape of a scarf is dictated by its intended final use. Scarves vary in design from a long rectangular shape created in varying widths for wrapping around the neck, to squares to tie around the head. The large surface area is one of the scarf's main advantages. A scarf can incorporate many different design features with some of the best-known examples including embroidery, printing and special weaves. The shawl, a variant of the scarf, reached Europe in the eighteenth century and was a fashionable accessory for both indoor and outdoor wear. Shawls were often woven with distinctive designs, including paisley, and at their most extreme were large enough to cover a crinoline.

Hermès have a long and famous history of creating silk printed scarves. Each Hermès scarf is complicated to make, even down to the printing process used whereby each colour is left to dry for up to a month until each one has been applied and all are then hand finished along the edge.

Before you begin thinking about designing a scarf, start by deciding upon the end requirement. Consider how the wearer would wear the item; would it be sported around the neck, across the shoulders or over the head? Creating a scarf using natural fibres will prove to be most comfortable for the wearer, with fur possibly the warmest. Texture within a scarf's design can be both aesthetic and ergonomic. Using a chunky knitting technique or padding can add bulk. Using synthetic fabric that is pleated or woven with a honeycomb structure is a useful method for trapping heat in the air pockets.

A tie is simply a piece of fabric that is wound around the neck and then tied or tucked into another garment. An early version of the tie can be traced back to the seventeenth century when Croatians would commonly wear a piece of fabric, a 'croat', tied around the neck. The French corrupted the word 'croat' to 'cravat', which translates into English as 'tie'. The tie thus originated as a scarf, eventually gaining in popularity to become a male-dominated accessory throughout Europe and the rest of the world. Variations of the tie include the popular necktie and bow tie, which are worn as part of a uniform for school, the military or work.

Necktie

Neckties gained hugely in popularity in the twentieth century to become a staple part of men's wardrobes, and today represent a common integral part of the male work uniform across a range of industries and sectors. However, it's true to say that the necktie has remained relatively unchanged for centuries. Not usually classified as an informal accessory, ties are often also associated with bringing prestige to the wearer during formal events.

The greatest variations in neckties over history have occurred with changes to the design of the fabric used to make them, including the weave, with the different use of materials such as jacquard, twill and satin employed, or with emblems woven into the design, for instance. Given its small surface area, the design used for the necktie can be bold or subtle, to either show off or to intimate something discreetly about the personality of the wearer.

Printed ties, for instance, may have serious or comical images. Striped ties in the United Kingdom slope down from the wearer's left shoulder to the right whilst in the United States, the lines run in the opposite direction. The width of the tie has also altered to suit fashion trends over the years, varying from the very wide (the so-called 'kipper' tie made fashionable in the 1970s, for instance) to the very narrow (such as the thin tie adopted by mods in the UK in the 1960s).

Bow tie

Simply a tie that has been tied into a bow, the bow tie is considered to epitomize the high point of men's formal wear with current trends dictating the size, colours and patterns that predominate in any given era. This accessory is associated with black- and white-tie events and is not typically seen as part of business attire. Bow ties are designed to be either self-tie or are pre-tied and held together with a clasp.

For centuries, timekeeping has been an obsession for many. Yet, the high cost of the complex mechanisms involved made the wristwatch an item available only to the privileged few in its early days. It wasn't until the advent of the twentieth century that the wristwatch became more widely available to the general masses. Today, this accessory ranges from the cheap to the very expensive with the finest masterpieces typically made by Swiss craftspeople.

9. Two distinctive watches worn on the same wrist, as seen in Vivienne Westwood's Spring/ Summer 2012 catwalk collection.

10–11. Over the centuries, watches have become highly developed with complex functions. Today, they represent the pinnacle of modern engineering, such as this white high-tech ceramic Chanel chronograph (10).

Design and construction

The first timepieces were developed as the size of clocks began to be reduced and eventually they were small enough to be worn on the wrist. Mechanical watches have a distinctive ticking sound and metal components were originally used. However, the constant wear on them caused the timekeeping to become inaccurate. Jewelled movements, using stones such as sapphires and rubies, improved the performance immensely, although these proved prohibitively expensive.

Digital watches were developed only with the help of a tiny battery that fits inside the watch. Much cheaper and lighter, these watches use a circuit board and display very accurate time for as long as the battery power continues. Quartz watches use the crystals that had already been a component feature in clocks; however, these developments took years of innovation and technological improvements before they became widespread.

The interior mechanism is the main limiting factor in wristwatch design, although the size and weight of the watch must also be considered carefully as each gender has different requirements. The design of the watch face can be basic, including only the essential dials for telling the time, or it may have many other dials to indicate other things like seconds and dive depth, for instance. Some rare examples of wristwatches have precious jewels and the finest metals incorporated into their design.

The wristwatch strap holds the accessory securely in place and many types are manufactured, including metal and ceramic bracelets; exotic leathers, such as shark and alligator are often used for bespoke and high-end wrist pieces; whilst plastic tends to prove a practical and popular material for sports watches.

168/169
168/169

9

10

11

Ties > Wristwatches > Belts
Ties > Wristwatches > Belts

Long since associated with a specific task, exquisite examples of belts from the Bronze Age have been unearthed that show that these accessories were never purely functional pieces.

Useful and suitable for both genders, a belt consists of a strap of material and is primarily designed to hold a garment in place. The most popular type of belt consists of a metal buckle and a leather strap with several holes with which the wearer can adjust the belt to the correct size. Belts are generally threaded through belt loops on trousers, skirts and dresses, although they may also be worn on the outside of garments to provide definition and silhouette to a look.

Styles of belts

Baldric, brez, contour, cummerbund, obi, sash, St. Tropez and webbed.

12–13. Belts for men are typically discreet and are the unsung hero of functional accessories. These examples by Coeur blend easily with the stylish outfits, not intruding on the daring colours or shirt patterns – thereby fulfilling a practical accessory's primary duty.

12

13

Design and construction

Today, belts have become statement accessory pieces in the fashion industry. Leather is the most important material in the construction of belts because of its strength and flexibility. Natural and synthetic materials such as plastic, vinyl and fabric are, however, also commonly used.

Length and width determine the design of a belt. A wider belt will have a larger surface area and will need to accommodate the waist, and so may require careful cutting in order to follow the contours of the body.

Use of a buckle offers the designer an opportunity to create an impact or statement with the accessory. The design of the buckle can also work to make it a special feature, with many designers using this piece of hardware for special logos and finishes, such as the insertion of precious stones. Ornate buckles with incorporated design features must also be able to perform an important function, however; whatever the design of the belt and buckle, they must both be able to withstand the continual pressure and stress exerted by the daily use of the wearer.

Cutting pieces of leather requires precision and care because long patterns can easily be distorted during this process. The leather strap must be carefully cut by hand to avoid blemishes; smaller pieces should be stamped out using a die. Backing pieces are then glued or sewn (or a combination of both) to the leather for strength. Holes are punched at regular intervals and finally the buckle is attached to hold the belt securely in place.

14

Fabric belts follow a similar method but require heavy backing material to create stiffness or a heavy woven strap that will enable them to withstand force of use. Any intended special design features, such as embellishment, are then added before the hardware is attached. Always carefully consider whether the design features will interfere with the use of the belt and whether the added embellishments are likely to weaken the overall structure of the material over time, and so affect the final outcome or success of the design.

14. A glowing neon leather belt contrasts sharply with the subdued tones that characterized Burberry's Spring/Summer 2011 collection.

Wristwatches > **Belts** > Gloves

Gloves are worn both as fashion accessories and as functional items designed to provide warmth to the wearer. Historically, gloves were an important accessory for the higher classes and royal courts, as well as for many industries that need to protect workers' hands from potential damage from machinery or labour. Today, the sportswear market also includes gloves as a major accessory, as they provide athletes with better grip and the ability to withstand impact.

15. Classic black leather opera gloves from the Dior Spring/ Summer 2011 haute couture collection, which combine the elegance of the 1940s with a modern burlesque twist.

16. Elbow-length leather glove with a floral appliqué in sparkling sequins by Lanvin (Autumn/ Winter 2011).

15

Design and construction

16

For many centuries, women's gloves were made from delicate fabrics and leather, and were designed to both indicate a woman's social status and to restrict the hand from manual work. Most prominent in the nineteenth and twentieth centuries, the use of gloves as an indicator of social standing has fallen out of cultural currency; today, they are generally used purely to keep the hands warm or for major social occasions.

The design of this accessory demands flexibility because of the important motor functions of the hand. Gloves vary greatly in length, shapes and thicknesses, from the large and bulky to the very slender that fit the wearer's fingers snugly.

Before beginning to think about the design of your gloves, consider carefully the protection and security needs that the design must offer the wearer. The design of the glove must accommodate both the hand and curve of the fist, allowing space for flexibility. The width of the cuff edge will depend on whether the glove needs to be wide enough to fit around, or narrow enough to fit under the sleeve. Commercial men's gloves are generally short to the wrist or long to the mid-forearm. Women's gloves have a wider variety of lengths, especially when it comes to close-fitting evening gloves, which include the matinee (which cover up to the wrist), the elbow (which cover the elbow area), or very long opera lengths (which cover the arm up to the bicep).

Begin construction by measuring the hand at the fullest part around the knuckles but not including the thumb. Measure the tip of the middle finger to the base of the hand to determine the length.

Selecting the correct materials is crucial to constructing gloves. Leather is one of the most popular materials for use with gloves because of its strength and flexibility. Gloves made from knitted fabrics, or those that are knitted in one piece, offer the closest fit.

Sewing requires extra care in order not to stretch pieces out of shape. There are two main sewing methods used when constructing gloves. An inseam involves sewing the gloves with the right sides together before turning them inside out so that all the seams remain hidden from view; although this method produces the most bulk. To reduce bulk, the pique seam can be used; this overlaps one raw edge over another before sewing the material close to the edge.

Select the correct sewing method for the type of material that you are using. Leather does not fray, therefore the pique seam is most suitable with this material; any fabric that frays will require an inseam. All other raw edges are then finished off, including the cuff, and the finished glove is placed on a form for final pressing.

Sustainable design

Sustainable design refers to the process of creating accessories in a way that has no, or a low impact on the ecological and social environment that surrounds you both locally and globally. Designing accessories from reused accessories and recycled materials provides a starting point and eventually an endpoint to the life cycle of the pieces that you create.

Objectives and learning outcome

To reduce waste before, during and after the production processes by using by-products from the industry or renewable sources of energy. Developing accessories through the use of smarter design in this way will generate a cleaner future for the industry.

Design task

Create new designs by collecting accessories that have reached the end of their useful life. Break down the accessories and take out all the useful components, including the hardwear, leather and fabric from bags and footwear, and reuseable materials from millinery, as well as separating metals and stones from jewellery.

Recondition the materials by cleaning any dirty residue from them, then take inspiration from the remaining components. Consider the limitations of the materials in front of you. Next, design a range of small accessories. Use the construction techniques introduced earlier by piecing together soft textiles or leather to create new fabric. Reusing metal and stone is more commonplace for jewellery design. Using metal that has been reshaped in high heat or stones that have been re-cut and polished brings a new dimension to small accessories such as belts and eyewear.

Materials
Produce accessories from materials that have a low impact on the environment. Use non-toxic man-made synthetics that break down and disperse easily, or natural non-synthetic organic materials, which are free of harmful pesticides, chemicals and hormones.

Design
Closing the design, production and use life cycle of your designs by producing reusable or recyclable accessories will mean that the products created will be more durable, so leading to fewer replacements.

Energy
Producing accessories using an efficient source of energy has a direct impact on the environment. Smarter uses of energy can lower emissions and better design leads to lower energy consumption when the accessory is in use.

17–19. Fabric, and tie and bow tie designs by Coeur for Emma Ashford that use cheerful colours and patterns to provide effective examples of sustainable design.

Small accessories

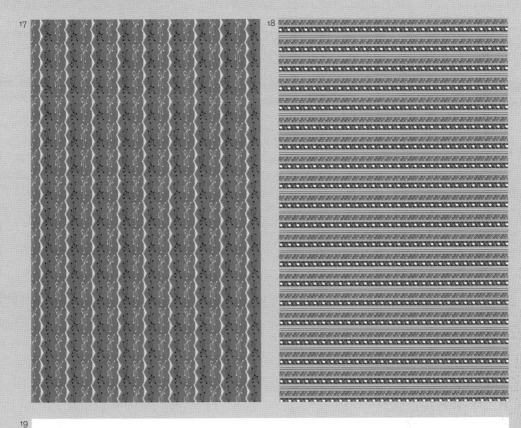

17

18

19

cœur

cœur & Emma Ashford Collaborative Project - Tie Designs

Claire Goldsmith

The world's most sophisticated and iconic sunglasses and spectacles are from a family with a long tradition of influential designers, which have a long list of followers including royalty and celebrities. Claire Goldsmith has brought forward the most innovative and iconic pieces to firmly establish a new generation of fresh eyewear designs for the future with her label CG Eyewear.

What is the history of Claire Goldsmith?

I am the great-granddaughter of one of the most iconic eyewear designers and brands, Oliver Goldsmith (est. 1926). In 2006, I instigated the reintroduction of the OG vintage archive, re-releasing many of the company's most iconic eyewear designs spanning the 1940s through to the 1980s. The success of this confirmed my passion to make some of the world's most expressive and well-made eyewear. In 2009, I launched my own collection – CG: Claire Goldsmith. With the support of the young and passionate design team I've got working with me here we have created a brand new contemporary eyewear line with my debut collection being aptly named 'Legacy'.

I felt very much like eyes were on me, waiting to see if I could actually design, innovate and create new frames and styles of my own rather than just remaking tried and tested OG archive designs. I think to be taken seriously in this industry you need to push forward with new ideas and not just look back at the past. You need to show that you are able to create and not just recreate.

21

22

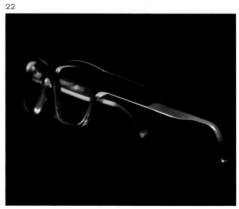

Small accessories

Where does your inspiration originate?

I'm sure it's obvious, but my inspiration originates from my family, my heritage – I am incredibly lucky to have such an expansive and extensive back catalogue of inspiration – in fact an entire attic full! Saying that, people are what inspire me the most, when travelling, walking along the street – everywhere you go, you see people wearing eyewear; I look at what works, what doesn't, I look at their face shape, how the frame fits. Also, angles and lines on other design-led products; eyewear can be inspired just as much from a piece of furniture as it can from the angle of a person's face.

What is the design process at Claire Goldsmith?

I'm emphatic that great brands communicate through great design and high quality. As such, none of my collections carry any outlandish logos or embellishments. Instead, contoured temples and defined lines are the signature style of CG: LEGACY. I tend to try and keep the collection balanced, so that there is something for everyone in terms of shape – round eyes, oval eyes, square eyes.

I like balance and therefore also try to keep the collection split evenly for men and women. Five years in the making, and myself and the team here have developed exquisite production techniques, strong design ideas and a deep passion for making the best eyewear in the world. CG: LEGACY really is set apart from anything currently on the market and this is just the beginning of what we hope will become a powerful and meaningful brand for decades to come.

How is the colour palette compiled?

We work with Italian acetate specialists Mazzucchelli who produce some of the strongest and most beautiful acetates in the world. I sit with the design team and start the process of choosing colourways from all the hundreds of colour options. Black and dark tortoiseshell frames will always be popular; they are classics, and usually each style is made in both these colours. In regards to new colourways, like most designers we are inspired by trends, fashion, art and our own inspiration and instinct. I also like to try and make acetate combinations that are unique to us using lamination of materials to create totally new colourways exclusive to our brand.

23

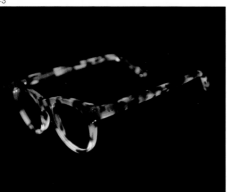

24

Claire Goldsmith

Why is the archive important?

Twice a year we dive into the vintage archive and piles of old design notepads and sketches to find new frames to launch for OG Sunglasses. The reassurance of knowing we have access to beautifully styled, well-proportioned frames is unique and the OG sunglasses collection is an opportunity to celebrate our heritage and reintroduce these incredible frames to this generation.

I see OG as the parent brand to my own brand – CG Eyewear – which is modern, new and adventurous, but with the depth and knowledge that OG has taught it. OG is a retrospective brand with a heritage set firmly in the past. It is like a guiding light but it is not the future. It can't be. The future has to be carried by a new generation and CG: Claire Goldsmith is a name that we fully intend to represent the Goldsmith family in eyewear in decades to come.

How do you develop a range?

Compared to others, we are still a small company and a relatively unknown brand – it's a big world out there. Our range is being built slowly but surely – with perhaps a maximum of ten styles being developed a year, currently there are approximately 30 styles in our range whereas mass-market brands can have over 100. This allows us the time to develop each frame with astute care and consideration.

We establish a theme for the collection, one tool we use is the contoured temple – this is something that follows through every CG frame so although frames are different, the shaping and beautiful angling of the temple is quite unique to CG. I tend to try and focus on traditional principles, but hope that in doing so I can push the boundaries of classic design and create some really special eyewear.

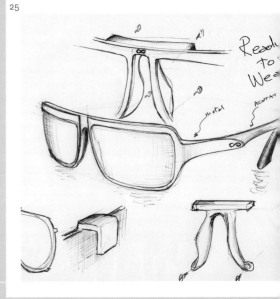

25

Why is manufacturing in England important?

Manufacturing in England is so important for many reasons. Firstly, there is the historical relevance; we are a British brand, and originally everything used to be made in England. Unfortunately, there aren't the means to manufacture to the scale we produce for our ready-to-wear collection in England, but this is exactly the reason we can produce our bespoke collection here – it allows us to support a dying art and craftsmanship that used to be thriving in this country, but now only a handful of incredibly talented people are keeping these skills and techniques alive, and we're very proud to be able to put our brand in their hands.

Small accessories

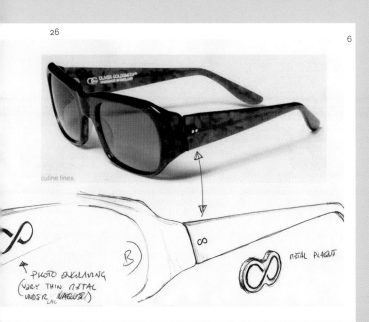

26

6

21–4. Claire Goldsmith's clever use of contrasts brings together heritage and contemporary influences for her spectacle frame designs.

25–6. Design development shows the careful consideration taken for each component that is used for the frames – which represent a triumph both of function and style.

What can you learn from making bespoke pieces?

We follow the same tried and tested technique of Oliver Goldsmith all those years ago. All glasses may look alike but how they are made makes all the difference. What can we learn? We learn about people – what they like and what they want from a product, as well as patience and craftsmanship in the artists who make these frames. Mass-produced can never and will never replicate something that has been inspired, designed and created by a person and their skill.

What inspires you most when working on collaborative projects?

Collaborative projects are something we only commit to when it's with a brand or project that we believe in – so essentially it is the partner who must inspire us. We must believe and share in their vision, and once that has been established we can move forward with the design process.

Why are spectacles and sunglasses an important fashion accessory?

The answer to this is simply that they sit on your face; the most prominent feature of your body – the feature everyone looks at day in and day out – why would you ever consider wearing a frame that didn't make the most of your personality and style? Eyewear doesn't need to follow trends, fashion can be frivolous and change too quickly, but with so many incredible brands out there making such interesting frames, I guarantee there is a frame out there for everyone.

Christina Brodie

27

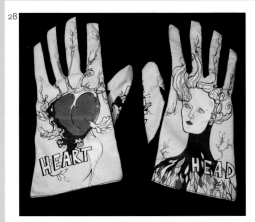

28

27–31. Christina Brodie's gloves are inspired by wide-ranging influences. With a joyful mix of colours and patterns, each pair of gloves tells a tale of reactions, emotions and feelings experienced by the designer.

Studying fashion and textiles before garden and landscape design, Christina Brodie has developed a unique signature style of gloves design. She brings tremendous energy to her work and reconciles a broad range of creativity to demonstrate her many accomplishments in the design and construction of bespoke gloves.

How do you start your research?

My research actually starts from a definite image, in my mind, of how the final product should look. I then go about selecting images, materials and methods, which will enable me to create that end result. I rarely arrive at an end result by accident. I always have a very strong idea of what I want to achieve from the outset. Depending on the complexity, size and requirements of the project, I may do a great deal of research, or I may do very little.

Where does your inspiration originate?

My inspiration comes from anything and everything in the world around me – stories, films, music, nature and philosophy. Those reactions, those emotions, those feelings that I experience are then translated into something with strength, dynamism, richness and forward-moving intent. I don't necessarily need to make a visual record of the subject matter for reference. I will take a mental photograph, unless the subject is particularly complex to grasp visually, and may need backing up with sketches or photographs in order to fix it in my mind. I am musical, and I do much the same thing when creating music. I mentally photograph the qualities of sounds that I hear.

What is your design process?

Sometimes the design process is very simple. I might make a very rough, tiny thumbnail sketch, from which I am able to create the product or object, and from which I can usually replicate proportions surprisingly accurately – this tends to be when I am creating more personal artwork.

Small accessories

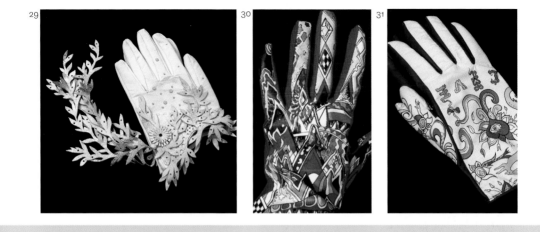

29   30   31

At other times, I may need to do extensive research, making moodboards or files crammed with visual and textile materials. For example, following discussions with a client, I might produce a series of highly detailed sketches from which a final model would be selected.

The fit of gloves tends to be more personally felt than with other garments due to a) their small size, and b) the great variety of hand shapes and sizes. Fit is very strongly affected by the fabrics chosen. There is considerable variety in stretch even in different parts of an individual leather skin, for example. Therefore, the design process involves a great deal of toile making and garment testing in final fabrics prior to creation of the master pattern.

How do you source your materials?

I don't produce to a large scale, but rather make one-offs or small runs of product. I don't buy in bulk, but rather source my materials and components from suppliers who are happy to sell small quantities to designer-makers, either by mail order or through retail outlets.

These are often small businesses themselves, and it is good to support each other in this way. Working on a small scale like this is also healthier for the environment. Inevitably there is always excess material left over at the end of a project, and I keep this to use in other projects. I am conscious of wastage and keen to avoid it.

Why are gloves becoming increasingly popular again as a fashion accessory?

I think interest in all manner of fashion accessories has grown substantially over the last two decades. But I think it is also the concept of 'fashion design as art' that has fuelled this boom. Millinery indubitably led the way, with superstar milliners such as Stephen Jones and Philip Treacy. There is no reason why gloves should not follow suit!

Gloves may also be a very good way of promoting designer labels (when endorsed by entertainers such as Lady Gaga) at a fraction of the price of a conventional designer garment.

Albrizio, A. and Lustig, O. (1999)
Classic Millinery Techniques:
A Complete Guide to Making and Designing
Today's Hats
Asheville: Lark

Allen, C. (2001)
The Handbag: To Have and to Hold
London: Carlton

Burch, M. (2002)
The Ultimate Guide to Skinning and Tanning:
A Complete Guide to Working with Pelts, Fur
and Leather
Connecticut: The Lyons Press

Couldridge, A. and Parry Crooke, C. (1980)
The Hat Book
London: Batsford

Gerval, O. (2009)
Fashion Accessories
London: A. & C. Black

Greenlees, K. (2005)
Creating Sketchbooks for Embroiderers and
Textile Artists
London: Batsford

Johnson, A. (2002)
Handbags: The Power of the Purse
New York: Workman Publishing

Macrae, S. (2001)
Designing and Making Jewellery
Marlborough: Crowood

McDowell, C. (1992)
Hats: Status, Style and Glamour
London: Thames and Hudson

McDowell, C. (2003)
Manolo Blahnik
Phoenix: Wiedenfeld Nicholson

McGrath, J. (2010)
The New Encyclopedia of Jewellery
Making Techniques
Kent: Search Press Ltd

O'Hara Callan, G. (1998)
The Thames & Hudson Dictionary
of Fashion and Fashion Designers
London: Thames and Hudson

O'Keefe, L. (1996)
Shoes: A Celebration of Pumps,
Sandals, Slippers and More
New York: Workman Publishing

Schwebke, P. and Krohn, M. (1970)
How to Sew Leather, Suede, Fur
London: Simon & Schuster Inc

Tain, L. (2010)
Portfolio Presentation for Fashion
Designers: 3rd Edition
New York: Fairchild

Tallon, K. (2008)
Digital Fashion Illustration
London: Batsford

Thaarup, A. and Shackell, D. (1957)
How to Make a Hat
London: Cassell

Tortora, P. (2003)
The Fairchild Encyclopedia
of Fashion Accessories
New York: Fairchild Publications

Vass, L. and Molnár, M. (2006)
Handmade Shoes for Men
Cologne: Könemann

Warren, G. (1987)
Fashion Accessories: Since 1500
London: Unwin Hyman

Wilcox, C. (2008)
Bags
London: V&A

Worthington, C. (1996)
Accessories
London: Thames and Hudson

©www.gorunway.com: 003, 008–09, 013, 015, 016–17, 018, 021, 035, 039, 040, 052–53, 063, 069, 084–85, 106–07, 118–19, 121, 122, 124–25, 131, 134–35, 140–41, 144–45, 148–49, 160–61, 163, 169, 172

©V&A images: 010–11, 038, 043, 058

©Catwalking: 019, 020, 026, 033, 034, 042, 051, 068, 142–43, 164–65, 171, 173

©Arnoldo][Battois: 014, 090–93

©Lara Bohinc: 027

©Michelle Lowe-Holder: 031, 150–153 (photography: ©Polly Penrose)

©Scott Wilson: 032, 072–75 (photography: ©Antonio Marguet)

©Georgina Martin: 034, 036–37, 056

©Stephen Jones: 040–41, 043, 064, 081–83, 098, 108–09 (lookbook photography: Peter Ashworth; millinery work rooms photography: ©Maria Eisl; all other images used courtesy of Stephen Jones Millinery)

©Philip Treacy: 044–49 (portrait of Philip Treacy, photography: ©Kevin Davies)

Jody Parchment: 054–55, 146–47 (photography: ©Arron Dunworth)

©Getty images: 058

Elin Melin: 060, 070–71

Kat Marks: 065, 067, 105, 133 (photography: 11–12 ©Saty + Pratha Photography; 13: ©Paul Hine Photography, millinery by Niamh Flanagan)

Hattie Hignell: 066, 078–79 (photography: ©Montana Lowry)

Heather Stable: 076–77

©Claire Goldsmith: 086–87, 176–79

All work and images property of Lee Mattocks: 088, 100–01, 144

Images courtesy of Cookson Precious Metals: 089, 096–97, 099

©Marloes ten Bhömer: 110–11, 136–39

©Beatrix Ong: 114–17

©Bill Amberg: 126–29

©Justin Smith Esq: 156–59

©PYMCA: 162

All rights reserved to Coeur Ltd.: 167, 170; ©Emma Ashford: 175

©Christina Brodie: 180–81

Alloy
A mixture of metals which enhance the properties of each to create a stronger material.

Base metal
A non-precious metal, such as copper and iron.

Bespoke
A made-to-order accessory.

Bias
The diagonal 45° degree angle from the warp threads of a woven fabric.

Biotechnology
Manufacturing products using living organisms and bio-processes.

Blemish
A mark, stain, imperfection or flaw on a piece of leather or skin.

Block
The base pattern of an accessory from which many other styles originate.

By-product
A material that derives from another origin and not purposefully intended for accessories design.

Canvas
A stiff fabric used to provide foundational support or weight to softer materials.

Cast
To form a piece of an accessory using a mould.

Classic
A style of accessory which remains popular over time.

Cobbler
A person who repairs footwear, rather than designing and manufacturing it.

Colourways
One of several different combinations of colours in which a given pattern or design is printed.

Commercial
Mass-produced accessories.

Components
The separate pieces of functional pattern and decorative features that make up the finished accessory.

Cord
A type of rope available in different thicknesses, which is used as a trimming or decorative feature.

Die
An outline of a shape in metal used to stamp out pattern pieces in leather or into several layers of fabric.

Dyes
Synthetic or natural chemicals that are used to add colour to materials before or after production of the accessory.

Embellishment
Decorative feature incorporated into the design of the material or layered onto the accessory.

Emboss
An image stamped onto the material that shows on both sides.

Fashion
A highly seasonal accessory design that is usually not repeated.

Finish
A specific type of technique, including stitching, edging and surfacing, used to complete an accessory.

Flux
A substance mixed with a solid to lower its melting point, used especially in soldering and brazing metals or to promote vitrification in glass or ceramics.

Form
A shape in which fabric, metal or material is formed.

Gild
To cover an object or accessory with gold.

Gores
Triangular inserts that are stitched together to form a sectional crown.

Grain
The direction of the threads in a woven fabric both lengthways and widthways.

Handle
The feel of goods, especially textiles, when handled. Some fabrics, such as silk, have a softer handle than do others, such as wool.

Hardware
Main solid functional components, such as frames for bags and fastenings.

Hat-block
A traditional tool used for moulding and shaping the structure of a hat during the design stage, typically made from wood or polystyrene.

Imitation
A reproduction of a style of accessory, image, texture or surface.

Inclusions
Most stones, including diamonds, contain inclusions or flaws that exist in various forms, exterior and interior. Inclusions are also classified in the manner in which they were formed.

Interfacing
A woven, knitted or felted fabric used to support a variety of materials.

Jeweller
A person who designs and constructs jewellery.

Last
A wooden form of a specific shoe type, style and size.

Leather
A material made from the skin of an animal by tanning or a similar process.

Life cycle
The length of time over which an accessory piece is designed to last.

Lining
A soft piece of fabric on the inside of an accessory used to give a neat finish and conceal the construction details.

Lockstitch
The most popular type of straight stitch with two interlocking threads used to hold layers of materials together securely.

Malleable
A metal's ability to be rolled, pressed or hammered without fracturing.

Milliner
A person who creates hats and caps.

Natural
Fibres created by plants, protein or living organisms.

Pattern
A paper template for a specific area of an accessory with markings to show cutting, placement and construction details.

Pickle
An acidic solution for cleaning blemishes and stains from metal surfaces during and after construction.

Polish
To create a high shine on a metal surface.

Print
Refers to several methods of printing techniques, including rotary, screen- and digital printing, used to transfer a specific design onto fabric and leather.

Production
The manufacturing process of an accessory that has developed through all the stages involved, including design and prototyping.

Prototype
A mock-up or trial piece used to check for scale, shape and size, and to correct any faults before final production.

Provenance
The place of origin or earliest known history of an object.

Rapid prototyping
This refers to a group of techniques used to quickly fabricate a scale model of a physical part or assembly using three-dimensional computer-aided design (CAD).

Recycling
A process whereby useful surplus materials, or the useful materials within the finished accessory pieces, are utilized in the creation of other products.

Residue
A chemical, material or dirt left behind during the production processes that needs to be cleaned from the finished accessory.

Scale
The proportional graduated sizes of an accessory.

Shape
The outline of an accessory.

Sinamay
A type of straw/natural fibre made from a plant (musa textilis) of the Philippines. It is usually dyed and stiffened and is mainly used in the production of hats and fascinators.

Sustainable
The ability to create accessories without the depletion of natural resources.

Synthetic
Usually a material made from man-made fibres, components or fabric.

Tempering
A process of softening metal with heat to reduce the brittleness of cold metal.

Texture
Characterized by the roughness or smoothness of a three-dimensional surface.

Toiles
An early version of a finished garment made up in cheap material so that the design can be tested and perfected.

Trim
The surface and edge decoration or functional fastening on an accessory.

Upcycling
Reusing an unwanted accessory by refashioning it into a useable product.

Warp and weft
The warp and weft are the basic constituents of all textiles. In weaving, the warp refers to the threads arranged on the loom, under which other threads (the weft) are passed to make a piece of cloth.

Shops and suppliers

Leather

A. W. Midgley & Sons
www.awmidgley.co.uk

Jewellery components, metals and stones

Cookson Gold
www.cooksongold.com

Parts for bags

Cox The Saddler
www.saddler.co.uk

Art and design supplies specialists

Fred Aldous Ltd.
www.fredaldous.co.uk

Synthetic leather

IPEL SRL
www.ipelsrl.it

Industry sewing, cutting, pressing and fusing machines

J. Braithwaite & Co. Ltd.
www.sewingmachinery.com

Fabric and haberdashery

John Lewis
www.johnlewis.com

Kleins [haberdashers]
www.kleins.co.uk

Laser-cutting specialists

Laser Cutting Services
www.lasercutit.co.uk

Trimmings, materials, haberdashery and notions

MacCulloch & Wallis
www.macculloch-wallis.co.uk

Pattern cutting and presentation equipment

Morplan
www.morplan.com

Leather

Pittards
www.pittardsleather.co.uk

Silk

Pongees
www.pongees.co.uk

Fur

Saga Furs
www.ffs.fi

Fabric

Whaleys (Bradford) Ltd.
www.whaleys-bradford.ltd.uk

Trade shows

Global Sourcing Fair:
Fashion Accessories
www.globalsources.com

London Fashion Week
www.londonfashionweek.co.uk

Première Vision
www.premierevision.com

Pure London
www.purelondon.com

Spring Fair International
www.springfair.com

Trend forecasting

Mudpie
www.mudpie.co.uk

Promostyl
www.promostyl.com

The Future Laboratory
www.thefuturelaboratory.com

Trend Stop
www.trendstop.com

WGSN
www.wgsn.com

Magazines

10

Bloom

Close-Up Accessories

Collezioni Accessori

Elle

Harper's Bazaar

i-D

L'Officiel

Love

Surface

Textile View

Vogue

Women's Wear Daily

Index

This book has been a huge investment in time, effort, skill and knowledge of all those who patiently answered my questions, offered advice and contributed their work.

My first and biggest thanks, with all my admiration, goes to Richard Craig, for all his support, the millions of things he does everyday to make my life easier and most importantly, his ability to make me laugh all the time. Thank you.

Special thanks must go to my extraordinarily talented friend Georgina Martin for her constant support in my many projects and ideas.

Colette Meacher, my patient editor, deserves a big thank you for gently guiding me through the writing and editing process.

An extra special thanks must go to the brilliant designer Lee Mattocks who has helped me throughout this book with his contributions and connections for which I am very grateful. Thank you to all the contributors – Peter Jeun Ho Tsang, Elin Melin, Hattie Hignell, Jody Parchment, Kat Marks, Heather Stable, Maria Eisl, Caroline Herz, Carly Wraeg and Nick Martin.

Thank you to all the designers who gave up their time to provide a valuable contribution to the book; Georgina Martin, Philip Treacy, Scott Wilson, Stephen Jones, Silvano Arnoldo, Massimiliano Battois, Beatrix Ong, Bill Amberg, Marloes ten Bhömer, Michelle Lowe-Holder, Justin Smith, Claire Goldsmith and Christina Brodie.

Thanks to my style advisors who have been my biggest influences: Lakshmi Basford, Janet Chan, Elytis Chan, Lorraine Johnson, Ashwin Johnson, Alexander King Chen and Carol Chan.

Thank you to all my colleagues at Manchester Metropolitan University for their advice and expertise, especially: Clare McTurk, Tasneem Sabir, Helen Rowe and Colin Renfrew.

Finally, my family – father, mother, sisters, brothers, nieces and nephews – thank you for unfailingly supporting my 'great' ideas.

Publisher's note

The subject of ethics is not new, yet its consideration within the applied visual arts is perhaps not as prevalent as it might be. Our aim here is to help a new generation of students, educators and practitioners find a methodology for structuring their thoughts and reflections in this vital area.

AVA Publishing hopes that these **Working with ethics** pages provide a platform for consideration and a flexible method for incorporating ethical concerns in the work of educators, students and professionals. Our approach consists of four parts:

The **introduction** is intended to be an accessible snapshot of the ethical landscape, both in terms of historical development and current dominant themes.

The **framework** positions ethical consideration into four areas and poses questions about the practical implications that might occur. Marking your response to each of these questions on the scale shown will allow your reactions to be further explored by comparison.

The **case study** sets out a real project and then poses some ethical questions for further consideration. This is a focus point for a debate rather than a critical analysis so there are no predetermined right or wrong answers.

A selection of **further reading** for you to consider areas of particular interest in more detail.

Ethical: aware-
ness/
reflect-
ion/
debate

Working with ethics

Introduction

Ethics is a complex subject that interlaces the idea of responsibilities to society with a wide range of considerations relevant to the character and happiness of the individual. It concerns virtues of compassion, loyalty and strength, but also of confidence, imagination, humour and optimism. As introduced in ancient Greek philosophy, the fundamental ethical question is: *what should I do?* How we might pursue a 'good' life not only raises moral concerns about the effects of our actions on others, but also personal concerns about our own integrity.

In modern times the most important and controversial questions in ethics have been the moral ones. With growing populations and improvements in mobility and communications, it is not surprising that considerations about how to structure our lives together on the planet should come to the forefront. For visual artists and communicators, it should be no surprise that these considerations will enter into the creative process.

Some ethical considerations are already enshrined in government laws and regulations or in professional codes of conduct. For example, plagiarism and breaches of confidentiality can be punishable offences. Legislation in various nations makes it unlawful to exclude people with disabilities from accessing information or spaces. The trade of ivory as a material has been banned in many countries. In these cases, a clear line has been drawn under what is unacceptable.

But most ethical matters remain open to debate, among experts and lay-people alike, and in the end we have to make our own choices on the basis of our own guiding principles or values. Is it more ethical to work for a charity than for a commercial company? Is it unethical to create something that others find ugly or offensive?

Specific questions such as these may lead to other questions that are more abstract. For example, is it only effects on humans (and what they care about) that are important, or might effects on the natural world require attention too?

Is promoting ethical consequences justified even when it requires ethical sacrifices along the way? Must there be a single unifying theory of ethics (such as the Utilitarian thesis that the right course of action is always the one that leads to the greatest happiness of the greatest number), or might there always be many different ethical values that pull a person in various directions?

As we enter into ethical debate and engage with these dilemmas on a personal and professional level, we may change our views or change our view of others. The real test though is whether, as we reflect on these matters, we change the way we act as well as the way we think. Socrates, the 'father' of philosophy, proposed that people will naturally do 'good' if they know what is right. But this point might only lead us to yet another question: *how do we know what is right*?

You
What are your ethical beliefs?

Central to everything you do will be your attitude to people and issues around you. For some people, their ethics are an active part of the decisions they make every day as a consumer, a voter or a working professional. Others may think about ethics very little and yet this does not automatically make them unethical. Personal beliefs, lifestyle, politics, nationality, religion, gender, class or education can all influence your ethical viewpoint.

Using the scale, where would you place yourself? What do you take into account to make your decision? Compare results with your friends or colleagues.

Your client
What are your terms?

Working relationships are central to whether ethics can be embedded into a project, and your conduct on a day-to-day basis is a demonstration of your professional ethics. The decision with the biggest impact is whom you choose to work with in the first place. Cigarette companies or arms traders are often-cited examples when talking about where a line might be drawn, but rarely are real situations so extreme. At what point might you turn down a project on ethical grounds and how much does the reality of having to earn a living affect your ability to choose?

Using the scale, where would you place a project? How does this compare to your personal ethical level?

01 02 03 04 05 06 07 08 09 10

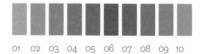

01 02 03 04 05 06 07 08 09 10

Your specifications
What are the impacts of your materials?

In relatively recent times, we are learning that many natural materials are in short supply. At the same time, we are increasingly aware that some man-made materials can have harmful, long-term effects on people or the planet. How much do you know about the materials that you use? Do you know where they come from, how far they travel and under what conditions they are obtained? When your creation is no longer needed, will it be easy and safe to recycle? Will it disappear without a trace? Are these considerations your responsibility or are they out of your hands?

Using the scale, mark how ethical your material choices are.

Your creation
What is the purpose of your work?

Between you, your colleagues and an agreed brief, what will your creation achieve? What purpose will it have in society and will it make a positive contribution? Should your work result in more than commercial success or industry awards? Might your creation help save lives, educate, protect or inspire? Form and function are two established aspects of judging a creation, but there is little consensus on the obligations of visual artists and communicators toward society, or the role they might have in solving social or environmental problems. If you want recognition for being the creator, how responsible are you for what you create and where might that responsibility end?

Using the scale, mark how ethical the purpose of your work is.

01 02 03 04 05 06 07 08 09 10   01 02 03 04 05 06 07 08 09 10

Working with ethics

One aspect of fashion design that raises an ethical dilemma is the way that clothes production has changed in terms of the speed of delivery of products and the now international chain of suppliers. 'Fast fashion' gives shoppers the latest styles sometimes just weeks after they first appeared on the catwalk, at prices that mean they can wear an outfit once or twice and then replace it. Due to lower labour costs in poorer countries, the vast majority of Western clothes are made in Asia, Africa, South America or Eastern Europe in potentially hostile and sometimes inhumane working conditions. It can be common for one piece of clothing to be made up of components from five or more countries, often thousands of miles apart, before they end up in the high-street store. How much responsibility should a fashion designer have in this situation if manufacture is controlled by retailers and demand is driven by consumers? Even if designers wish to minimise the social impact of fashion, what might they most usefully do?

Traditional Hawaiian feather capes (called 'Ahu'ula) were made from thousands of tiny bird feathers and were an essential part of aristocratic regalia. Initially they were red ('Ahu'ula literally means 'red garment') but yellow feathers, being especially rare, became more highly prized and were introduced to the patterning.

The significance of the patterns, as well as their exact age or place of manufacture is largely unknown, despite great interest in their provenance in more recent times. Hawaii was visited in 1778 by English explorer Captain James Cook and feather capes were amongst the objects taken back to Britain.

The basic patterns are thought to reflect gods or ancestral spirits, family connections and an individual's rank or position in society. The base layer for these garments is a fibre net, with the surface made up of bundles of feathers tied to the net in overlapping rows. Red feathers came from the 'i'iwi or the 'apapane. Yellow feathers came from a black bird with yellow tufts under each wing called 'oo'oo, or a mamo with yellow feathers above and below the tail.

Thousands of feathers were used to make a single cape for a high chief (the feather cape of King Kamehameha the Great is said to have been made from the feathers of around 80,000 birds). Only the highest-ranking chiefs had the resources to acquire enough feathers for a full-length cape, whereas most chiefs wore shorter ones which came to the elbow.

The demand for these feathers was so great that they acquired commercial value and provided a full-time job for professional feather-hunters. These fowlers studied the birds and caught them with nets or with bird lime smeared on branches. As both the *'i'iwi* and *'apapane* were covered with red feathers, the birds were killed and skinned. Other birds were captured at the beginning of the moulting season, when the yellow display feathers were loose and easily removed without damaging the birds.

The royal family of Hawaii eventually abandoned the feather cape as the regalia of rank in favour of military and naval uniforms decorated with braid and gold. The *'oo'oo* and the *mamo* became extinct through the destruction of their forest feeding grounds and imported bird diseases. Silver and gold replaced red and yellow feathers as traded currency and the manufacture of feather capes became a largely forgotten art.

Is it more ethical to create clothing for the masses rather than for a few high-ranking individuals?

Is it unethical to kill animals to make garments?

Would you design and make a feather cape?

Fashion is a form of ugliness so intolerable that we have to alter it every six months.

Oscar Wilde

AIGA
Design Business and Ethics
2007, AIGA

Eaton, Marcia Muelder
Aesthetics and the Good Life
1989, Associated University Press

Ellison, David
Ethics and Aesthetics in European Modernist Literature:
From the Sublime to the Uncanny
2001, Cambridge University Press

Fenner, David E W (Ed)
Ethics and the Arts:
An Anthology
1995, Garland Reference Library of Social Science

Gini, Al and Marcoux, Alexei M
Case Studies in Business Ethics
2005, Prentice Hall

McDonough, William and Braungart, Michael
Cradle to Cradle:
Remaking the Way We Make Things
2002, North Point Press

Papanek, Victor
Design for the Real World:
Making to Measure
1972, Thames & Hudson

United Nations Global Compact
The Ten Principles
www.unglobalcompact.org/AboutTheGC/TheTenPrinciples/index.html